Y

The Power of Foresight

To Chris and Kerry
Many blessings

Bill

Bill Allen

First Printing, 2018

ISBN 978-1724649324

Business Improvement Press
Barwood
Lower Warberry Road
Torquay
TQ1 1QP

www.businessimprovementpress.com

Cover design by Shape + Letter
www.shapeandletter.co.uk

Dedication

I dedicate this book to my wife Vicky who put up with me whilst I wrote it, to my great friend and training colleague Philip Avery who painstakingly edited it for me, to my father who was an outstanding role model to me and, finally, to my three children, Robert, Edward and Lily, who reminded me how often we use the word "Why" when we don't understand a decision.

Contents

Introduction

Why is Asking 𝕐 so powerful

Asking 𝕐 was a concept I birthed over a period of 25 years in business, both running, working in and consulting with businesses and business people.

I will not pretend that the idea of 𝕐 is new. We started doing it as children to great effect when our parents refused to give us what we wanted and every rebuttal on their part was met by the ever more intense *WHY*? If only we had, as adults, continued to use both the question and the passion behind it, then many situations in our life would definitely have been different.

Over the years there have been many headlines in the newspapers asking why situations happen. A classic newspaper cover is the stark photograph of a terrible disaster or murder and just the single word *Why*? In all cases these questions are asked after the event.

The concept of asking why is used in root cause analysis and was turned into a science by Sakichi Toyoda, (1867-1930), whose family went on to create the Toyota Car Company, with his development of the *5 Whys*. He felt that if you asked why up to five times you would get to the root cause of what is wrong in any given situation.

W Edwards Demming (1900-1993) famous for revolutionising car manufacture using the concept of Quality Management referred to the work of Toyoda when he said that "If you don't know how to ask the right questions, you discover nothing. It would seem that asking the *right* questions - knowing *what* to ask when you ask why - is essential for success when using the 5 Why technique.

Since both Mr Toyoda and Mr Demming died in the last century and both referred to the concept of asking why, how can I feel that I am birthing a new concept with asking 𝕐"?

All the research I have done into asking why has, with rare exceptions, shown that systems come into play after a situation has already occurred when, essentially, you are picking up the pieces and, in some cases, at a high financial or personal cost.

The reason I changed the "Why" to Y was not some clever way of having a unique title but was a way to separate it from the very valid processes of asking "why" after the event. With asking 𝕐 first and then the additional questions of "How, Who, When and What", I want to introduce you to the idea of asking many of the normal hindsight questions *before* the situation happens, either to stop it happening in the first place or to shape the way it will happen - using the power of *foresight.*

This technique allows you to take greater control of the future instead of the usual situation where the future controls you and you must react to the situations that have occurred.

Asking 𝕐 is the start of a journey and this book will help you decide if you should take that journey, and help you to start it.

Here are some reasons for using the concept:

- It could be that you have made major mistakes in

your life and you know that if you had asked the right questions before you made the decision things could have been different.

- It could be that you feel your ability to collect the meaningful data has never been one of your strong points.
- It could be you are facing challenges ahead and you want to properly prepare for them.
- It could be that you feel that things are OK but they could be better.
- It could be that you like to constantly update your abilities and want to know how this could help you.

This book will help you in all these areas and many more. All good consultants have used this technique instinctively over the years. People say that consultants charge money to find out information you already knew, which is true. However, without them, would you have thought to collect that information? Most people would not. The skill of a consultant is the ability to ask the right questions, the major question being to ask "Y is a situation the way that it is and does it need to alter?" By using this technique, you become your own consultant.

To help you put the concept into practice, I have not only described the technique but have also included chapters that show the application of it to many business and personal issues we face daily. You will not only see how the technique works but also pick up some very useful business tips in the process. Check out the contents page for the list of issues we will cover.

I hope this book will change the way you do things for the future. If it helps you, please write and tell me.

There are two great days in a person's life -- the day we are born and the day we discover why.

William Barclay
1907 – 1978
Author, radio and television presenter

Chapter 1

Asking 𝕐 - the concept

P eople are used to asking "Why" did something happen, or "Why" did it go wrong, or "Why" did we not meet expectations". However, in all those cases we are asking it after the fact, as a post mortem. The technique I am going to introduce differs in that it's key is to ask the question "Why" upfront in an effort to control the outcome and get the result we want so we do not have to look back and ask why we didn't get it. To differentiate, we are going to just use the letter 𝕐 when we are looking at a situation ahead of time.

The concept is remarkably simple to state - before you make a decision about a situation or if you want to understand the actions you should take:

Ask 𝕐

Then keep asking 𝕐 until you have exhausted all the questions you can come up with about the situation, issue or decision you have to make.

Clearly, the fact that the majority of the population has never used it shows it does not form part of our natural development nor is it taught to us during our education. Every business consultant knows it is the key to turning around any major issue within a business. First, we ask "why" did we get to where we are, and then 𝕐 should the changes we will be proposing be effective. After that we can get into "*What*" needs to be done, "*Who*" needs to be involved and "*How*" and "*When*" it should be done.

I must admit I can look back over the years and see many times in my life that I wish I had known this technique and used it, but then, as usual that is because we do seem to have the greatest ability to question ourselves and our actions either after the event or with the advantage of hindsight. To change that meant learning the skill of asking ⅄.

I remember one of the first times that I thought about the concept was when, as a General Manager for McDonald's, I was conducting an audit in one of the restaurants. As part of a team, I would stand by and watch the members of staff do their best to impress us with their service and standards of quality and cleanliness.

All was going fairly well when just as the day shift was finishing and the nightshift were due to take over, queues formed at the tills. Immediately everyone tried to kick into another gear knowing they would be timed on how long it took them to serve the customers.

The nightshift manager came onto the shift, saw the queues, panicked a little, and rushed to try and help the tills by assembling the orders for them, which would normally speed up the service. Unfortunately, in this case, it was a lack of cooked food that was the problem, not the speed of the service from the till operatives.

All the manager did was to ensure their scores were going to slip as he helped empty the production transfer bin, meaning now that none of the tills could sell anything. I remember thinking at the time, "That's not going to solve the situation"

- he needed to get into the kitchen and help them there, as they were running behind.

It was at that moment that I remember saying to myself why didn t he first ask Y the queues had formed and then analyse the facts momentarily before he jumped in to solve the problem as he saw it. There may have been many reasons why he didn't, probably keenness, nerves, or anxiety, to name but a few, but the reality is that the real reason was that he was not conditioned to do so. It had not become part of his nature to ask why a situation had developed and gain all the information he could before jumping in with a solution.

I am convinced that women are by nature better at this technique then man. In his great book, Men are from Mars and Woman are from Venus, John Gray illustrated how a woman likes to talk through a situation first, but get so frustrated with man as he is already trying to solve the problem before the woman feels she has properly discussed the situation.

I guess as a male of the species, I should ask Y can't I learn to keep my big mouth shut until my wife has finished what she is saying fully. It certainly would save on the arguments.

The problem is that we are emotional beings and we tend to act, or worse, react to situations through our emotions rather than with any real degree of logic. We can be quick to jump in, yet the situation often does not warrant or need such an instant response. At other times we get excited about a situation and we just keep seeing all the positives and fail to take into account, or make room for, the negatives. We see things that prove our current thinking, making it even harder to see alternatives that may not be as instantly attractive. Which is why we must also use our other diagnostic friends of "How,

Who, When, and What resources are needed.

As an example of the technique in action here are some classic Y work questions that are rarely asked:

Y do our customers buy from us?
Y do only some of my team take my direction?
Y can't we hire more talented people?
Y are we not making more profit?
Y don't I know what profit I am making?
Y does our advertising not produce better results
Y is delegating so difficult?
Y are some people always late for meetings?
Y does there seem to always be chaos at work?
Y isn't it as easy to do business anymore?

Y also works on a personal basis:

Y do I always have crushing deadlines?
Y is my desk always a mess despite all my efforts?
Y do I keep putting things off?
Y can't I say no?

So, what is the key? Stopping long enough to first ask Y that situation has arisen. This does not only have to be at a time of a crisis, although it is at times like that we really must stop to use the technique, but it should be used to challenge the status quo and this is where it becomes the powerful tool of a leader.

When I go to see a customer to help them develop their business, I go in armed with the technique. I accept nothing at face value until I have had the opportunity to challenge it with the concept .

Over the next chapters you will see some of the key areas where I use the technique to help develop the business, which I hope you will do the same for your business and later in the book I also look at the ways of using the technique on a personal basis, that you may find useful to use.

I would imagine since you started reading this you have already reflected on areas in your business or personal life where you could ask $\mathbb{Y}$, to take a better look at the current situation. If so, you are already starting the journey.

Asking $\mathbb{Y}$ on its own will not solve the problem. Once we have asked $\mathbb{Y}$ we will need to decide on a new course of action, we must then ask How we will achieve it, Who will be needed to achieve it, What time frames need to be set in place, and What resources we will need. We must first collect all the data we can and then use $\mathbb{Y}$ to challenge the data, helping us to see the clearer path.

However, a lot of times in our life we will not have the luxury of proper reflection; we will have to act in that moment. When that happens we must school ourselves to press the pause button long enough to ask $\mathbb{Y}$ is the situation the way it is, or what do I need to reflect upon before I can make a safe decision?

If you don't know where you are going, any road will get you there.

Lewis Carroll

Chapter 2

Holding an Ask 𝕐 meeting

If you have a major decision to make, or you have a new product idea, or maybe a major policy change you want to propose, then your first step should be to organise a 𝕐 meeting to consider all the aspects you should be asking 𝕐 about.

10 Steps to Running an Ask 𝕐 Meeting

1. Start by clearing your own thoughts, what I call the 'back of the envelope' technique. You start by writing down every aspect of the situation from your point of view, on the back of an envelope if you wish.

   You may have thought through problems before but not put them down on paper. Despite the apparent ease of just thinking a problem through, the reality is that we tend to think with the same part of our brain. If we do not do something to widen our access to other parts of the brain, we are limited to the knowledge we have stored there and may miss other information and even warnings that other parts of the brain can offer. I urge you to do your thinking on paper, as the action of writing engages motor functions which come from another part of the brain, usually the left side of the brain. Equally, the use of colours triggers other parts of the brain.

2. Break your list down into headings that you will need to look at more closely. This will form the basic structure of

the meeting. Don't hide these from the participants: send them out in advance and ask them to do their own   back of the envelope and bring it with them.

3. Select the individuals who will be at the meeting. Always work hard to balance the people at the meeting, so you don't have too many similar characters that might railroad the opinions of others. Also, dependent on the nature of the issue you will be discussing, you need to consider using different people within the hierarchy if it is a business, and the family or friends if it is not work related.

People see things from different perspectives and their challenging questions and insights could be just the thing needed to steer the issue safely through the potentially treacherous waters.

I am always surprised how people in different positions within the company can bring a fresh perspective to the session even if they are in an area that won't be involved.

4. Invite the person you didn t want to invite. You will probably know immediately what I mean by the person you didn t want to invite because you feared they would be a blockage to your idea.

The problem is that they are the very people you do need to invite when asking $\mathbb{Y}$ at the start, as you must ensure that you haven't over-looked an area through your enthusiasm for an idea or venture to succeed, and they may make the necessary challenge that could either improve the idea or (and this is sometimes the outcome) kill off the idea before it goes wrong on you.

5. Prepare the room properly. You need space, so people can walk around if they choose. Provide on-tap refreshments so that it doesn't break up the creativity of the meeting at a crucial moment to break for coffee. Take breaks when you have reached the end of an agenda item. Also ensure you have flip charts or whiteboards and multi-colour pens which can be used to either show who gave the suggestion with an assigned colour, or the addition of new thoughts to an existing list or mind map.

Have access to the internet so people can do some instant research on Google; this can save time in the future and trigger some new thoughts as well.

Depending on the strength of the issue, do not set a time limit and do ensure all distractions have been removed, especially phones.

6. Standard rules of brainstorming apply. This is not the time for filtering the thoughts, just the time to get them onto paper. Everyone must be encouraged to participate, and no idea is a bad one.

7. There are various concepts that can be used in brainstorming like Mind Mapping or Spider Diagrams which help keep the discussion from getting too linear.

8. You need a Chairperson to keep order. I would suggest it is not you due to your proximity to the concept.

9. Make sure all thoughts and ideas are transcribed and put into a Word document. This helps to focus your thinking when you later reflect on the concept.

10. Once you have assimilated all the information, you can draw your list of conclusions, and in almost all cases the path going forward will be clearer.

To first ask Ⲩ is one of the most crucial things that anyone should do before setting a course of action, and time spent in a Ⲩ meeting will help you avoid some of the pitfalls out there.

The rest of this book will give you ideas for your 'back of the envelope' sessions.

Section 1

Asking Y in Business

Don't aim to break the glass ceiling; aim to shatter it

Matshona Dhliwayo

Chapter 3

Ask 𝕐 to break the glass ceiling

On the financial side, we look at 𝕐 the profit is where it is and yet don't ask 𝕐 is the turnover at the level it is sitting at. Interestingly, I find that the turnover in most companies is around the point that the directors are aiming to achieve. I then ask them 𝕐 they are aiming for that level. It could be because of a lack of vision for more, but usually it is due to a glass ceiling that has set in, which makes everyone feel that they are probably doing the best they can be at this point. My experience has shown that this glass ceiling can be shattered by first asking 𝕐.

I worked with one company who had its turnover around the £11million mark for decades. Now they wanted to increase it by £5 million, primarily to fund the building of a new factory.

Certainly, their market place could easily accommodate it. I asked 𝕐 didn t they set a higher target? You could see the surprise on the face of the Managing Director. He was struggling with the concept of aiming for £5 million more, and here I was asking them to think bigger. I wouldn't have been surprised if at that point if he was questioning the wisdom of having me sit there asking them questions.

I persevered and asked him 𝕐 did he feel they couldn t do more? Well this stopped him. For ages, he sat there thinking about that question and then finally agreed that really there was nothing stopping them, other than not having thought about it before, and the need to get his head around it.

We looked at the market place and his market share would not have to grow that much. We looked at his site and it was big enough to add the necessary factories over the years to be able to produce it. We listed some of the obstacles, always remembering to ask, Ⓨ was it an obstacle? Ultimately, it boiled down to some simple areas like marketing and training, but the biggest challenge had already been overcome which was to raise the belief in the MD that it could be achieved. By asking Ⓨ it was a problem, we removed those mental obstacles one by one.

By the end of our time together. he had reworked his Mission to aim for a £30 million turnover within 20 years, with the first vision being a £5 million increase in four years. I went away believing it would be possible, that it was not unrealistic.

Ten months later I worked with them again and asked for an update. If they were hitting the newly selected target, then sales would have grown by a half a million at this point.

The Managing Director with the most triumphant of smiles said, "We got it." I congratulated him on being on target and well done on getting the extra half a million in sales. "Oh, no", he said, "We haven t got half a million, we have reached the extra five million!"As you can imagine we had a major celebration.

Now, I am not saying for one minute that asking Y delivered those five million of extra sales: that was achieved by a good sales and marketing campaign, training for the new staff, extra effort by their suppliers, etc. What asking Ⓨ achieved was to make them realise it was possible to aim for it, and this opened their thinking and led them to make the choices and decisions necessary to make it happen.

As you might guess, they no longer feel that taking the business to £30 million is a stretch of the imagination. Just recently, I have viewed some of their commercials. They had never advertised on television in their own right, and yet, now, with the confidence they feel for their business, they are reaching out to totally new markets.

It is interesting how, if you give a salesperson a target to hit, that target can become a glass ceiling. Ask for a thousand a day and the sales person will ultimately hit it. Ask for two thousand and, ultimately, they will hit that as well. So here is a thought for you: Y is the target set at one thousand in the first place?

Now, if you just arbitrarily raised the salesperson's target by double, it might demotivate them and they would not aim for it. However, raising it in smaller increments on a regular basis can achieve the same result without that risk.

So, like I asked the managing director, make sure you ask Y your targets are where they have been set.

What I want is to be number one

Steve Prefontaine
American Athlete 1951 – 1975

Chapter 4

Ask 𝕐 should Ichiban be our creed

Let's face it, unless you have heard this phrase before, you are probably thinking right now, "What on earth does it mean?" *Ichi* is the Japanese for 'one' and adding the numerical suffix *ban* changes the word to mean 'first'.

This was the goal Japanese companies set themselves after World War II, to be first in everything they did. Many achieved it, to the cost of manufacturing in other countries.

An internet search brings up a list of companies that have linked their product to the value of being first:

- Kirn Ichiban - Beer at its purest 100% malt
- Ichiban Clothing
- Ichiban International - Karate outfits and black belts
- Ichiban Noodle Bar - Glasgow
- Ichiban Sushi & Noodle Bar - London
- Ichiban 7 Brush Set - Take painting to the next level

The list reveals a varied range of companies using the Ichiban value of being first.

The question must be asked: 𝕐 can't your company or endeavours put you first? To answer this, you will have to ask 𝕐 you aren't ichiban now and how you can become it in your sector or activity.

"Perfection is our goal – Excellence will be tolerated"

J Yahl

Chapter 5

Ask 𝕐 isn't it perfect

We spoke about Mr Deming in the introduction to this book and his reflections on the work of Mr Toyoda of Toyota car fame. In this chapter, we are going to pay homage to W Edwards Deming, but also to Philip Crosby, and Joseph Juran, all of whom built on the work of Walter Shewhart who, whilst working at Bell Labs, first described the Plan-Do-Study- Act cycle (later to be known as the Shewhart Cycle) as part of Statistical Process Control which ushered in the concept of continuous improvement.

The understanding of quality is greatest in Japan but is growing apace in most commercial markets. It has had a resurgence with Six Sigma and Lean Manufacture, yet the fundamental principles have not changed.

The aim is to achieve a product with no defects and the only way to get there is to ask 𝕐 we want to design it that way, or 𝕐 is our production line set out the way it is, and 𝕐 we tolerate imperfection. Equally, we must do a post mortem and ask "why" did it go wrong; "why" are we getting these tolerance levels; "why" did it happen in the first place. Only then do we have a chance to deliver a product or service with zero defects.

I have had the great pleasure of working regularly with Vic Bromwich who was trained and worked for the Philip Crosby Organisation. Philip Crosby wrote the book *Quality is Free*.

I remember one time commenting to Vic that I had been to a

Mobile Home manufacturer and how the Managing Director had told me how they get around the tolerance issue of joining two 32-foot-long halves together. He had explained that they have to get the living room right as it is one big room across the two halves and the join would show if it was not perfect. However, they try not to have too many parallel lines at the other points where the two halves are joined together to mask the tolerances as they work their way down the house.

I felt that it was a sensible suggestion to use the design to solve the problem, to which Vic answered, "Why don't they just get the tolerances right - then they would have freedom of design".

Well, that hit me like a ton of bricks - it was so simple, yet it was clearly stating the obvious that the company making the homes had not taken it on board. Contrast that to the German house manufacturer, Huf Haus, who work to the minutest tolerances and who also build the house in a factory first. They ooze quality systems. At the end of the build on site, the job is not done till the vans and all the tool boxes are fully cleaned! We are lucky if our workers vacuum up after themselves.

One of the big problems in our efforts to achieve quality is that it requires a buy-in from senior management: without that, it will fail. Equally there has to be a genuine passion within the business for the effort to be expended to achieve 'zero defects', frequently hampered by the fact that people often have a problem with it, seeing it as a requirement and, therefore, an impossible goal to achieve, rather than seeing it as a process of a continuous reduction in the number of defects caused by the production process.

Now, it was easy when you had skilled craftsmanship where

they could set their own level of quality and the customer would buy accordingly. However, things became more complex with the onset of the industrial revolution and the advent of the production line. The production line allowed standardisation of output. Look at Henry Maudslay's precision screw cutting machine, and the Royal Navy block-making line of Maudslay and Marc Brunel that could produce 130,000 ships' blocks in a year. It was the application of standardised process control that really made the difference. Now we needed to get into quality control to monitor the outcome. This was very much an inspection process.

In time, we moved from quality control to quality assurance where quality engineering delivered a more consistent production process. No more Monday or Friday cars that weren't as good as the other days of the week. This was achieved by the introduction and use of Quality Circles, developed by Ishikawa at Kawasaki, extensively used by Toyota, and introduced to Europe by Joseph Juran

The natural progression was quality management with zero defects as the target and everyone within the company would be involved in achieving this outcome. Not just consistency but striving for the best outcome every time. In America, Philip Crosby popularised the phrase Total Quality Management or TQM, which became very big in the 80s and 90s.

I know that quality is a journey and that it never ends, but it does have a starting point and that is to ask Y are we going to do it that way, and will it give us the right outcome?

Let's go and ask everyone we work with, members of our family, our Church, our clubs, our sports club or of any hobbies we have, this simple question: Y do we do what we do in this way. In doing so, we are starting a process known as Kaizen, which is Japanese for *Kai* meaning 'change' and *Zen* meaning 'good'. In other words, changing for the good. This process was extensively used by Taiichi Ohno to raise the standards of production at Toyota. I can assure you that once you start asking Ⓨ you will be surprised by the answers you get.

*If someone can make a contribution
to the company, he feels important*

W Edwards Demming

Chapter 6

Ask Y don't we ask the staff

How can we improve where we are and what we do? Probably not too surprisingly, there is a question we must ask ourselves - Y are we doing what we do this way, can it be improved, and have we ever asked the opinion of the staff or team members?

I am always surprised by how little we expect from our staff in this area. How often do we ask the people who are doing it if there is a way that it could be done better? Sadly, the answer to this for most companies is that they don't think to do it and have no system for asking.

It is possible that you have the same jaded view as most when it comes to asking the staff. I certainly did when we first put in a suggestion box, mostly because we would find that most of the suggestions put in the box were anatomically impossible!

At that time, I was working with a major multi-national. To address this, we introduced a scheme that rewarded the staff if the idea, having gone through a panel, was felt to have merit. We had three levels of prizes, which in the great scheme of things were not worth an awful lot each. But when you sent in a suggestion, you received a letter from the chairman of the committee thanking you, whether or not you won a prize. This went down very well with the staff. Even better, though, for those who did win a prize, their idea was written up in the company newsletter that went out to 50,000 people. For those who are motivated by praise and recognition, this was worth more than any prize. Most people want the respect of their peers more than they want a cash incentive

What is so powerful about asking the staff is that they quite often come at a situation from a very different angle. They don't necessarily have the same mental constraints as those locked into a set way of doing things. The effectiveness of this can be seen in an example: At the time that one of the members of staff came up with the solution to a problem, I estimate that over 100,000 people had looked at it, all to no effect. You see, we were all coming at it from the same direction with the same mind-sets, which was the need for the staff member to do all the procedures 100% accurately or there would be a major mix up in the finished product and the customer would not get the product described on the outside of the box. We all felt the solution was better training.

This particular staff member, on the other hand, looked at the problem with fresh eyes and saw that the fault was in an early stage of the manufacturing process and that a change at that point would solve the issue.

The member of staff asked a simple question, 𝕐 didn't we get the mould changed so that it removed the issue. This simple approach of stepping back several stages in the manufacturing process was so obvious - once the staff member had suggested it!

Now, I thought that our ideas scheme was good until I heard about a Japanese firm that, instead of offering a prize, felt it was part of the duties of all staff members to suggest improvement, so much so that they built it into the annual objectives of the staff.

Each year they expected each member of staff to contribute ideas that were good enough so that at least 45% of them could be implemented. That, too, was part of the company goals, but was also very sensible because it demonstrated that not all ideas would be implemented, removing that feeling of "Well I gave them an idea and they didn't act on it."

With a staff of 120, how many ideas do you think they set as a goal? Maybe one a year per staff member, so 120 ideas, or maybe two a year giving you 240? What about one a quarter giving you 480? Could we manage one a month which is a whopping 1200? In the companies that I was originally trained in and which operated a suggestion box it was unlikely they would get even the 120, let alone 1200.

Amazingly, this firm set the goal at 2,000 and got it each year. That's right: 2000 annual improvement suggestions of which 45% were implemented, which equates to 900 improvements per year. I accept that in manufacturing this is a little easier as there are many processes that can be altered. But I have yet to work with a company that cannot significantly improve its systems and processes.

There is nothing more frightful than ignorance in action.

Johann Wolfgang von Goethe
Collected Works

Chapter 7

Ask Y don't we count the cost of ignorance

Ray Kroc, the President of McDonald s, was once asked how he could justify the amount of money he spent on training. As president of a public company, he had a duty to shareholders to maximise their investment, and it was clear that this was the opinion held by the person who challenged him to explain what they saw as profligate spending. Unfazed by this attack, Ray Kroc uttered the immortal line, "Before you count the cost of training, count the cost of ignorance."

Running the world s largest fast food restaurant chain, you would feel that he was an authority that you could bank on, and as a result companies would have emulated his training programmes to achieve the same level of success. Yet it staggers me how many companies spend huge amounts on advertising and then treat the customer to the responses of an untrained member of staff.

Why do we feel that we can run our businesses with untrained staff?

Dale Carnegie wrote back in the 1930s that companies spend large amounts of money acquiring premises, then more on fixtures and fittings, a large amount of money to stock the shop, and then none on training the staff to run this incredibly well kitted-out shop. Who hasn t been served by Saturday staff who don't know, and don't seem to be interested in, what they are selling and can't help you choose the product you need?

One of the outcomes of untrained staff is that bad habits run through the business creating inconsistent standards. Staff will find their own way to achieve a task either by copying someone or by trial and error. The first reinforces the bad habits, the second creates inconsistent standards.

It reminds me of the story of the man who came home from the butchers with a joint of ham. His wife asked him why he hadn't got the butcher to bone it. The husband replied that he didn't realise he should have done so, to which his wife responded, "We always get the butcher to cut the bone off the ham!" This is when he used our concept. He asked his wife 𝕐 did they get the bone cut off the ham.

His wife paused, thought for a while and then told him that it was because her mother had always done so. The husband felt he needed the answer, so he asked his mother in law the same question. She, too, paused for a while and then concluded that it was because her mother had done the same.

With curiosity raised to the full, he felt the only answer was to get onto his wife's grandmother and ask her the question, Y? Phoning up his wife's grandmother, he almost shouted down the phone, "Grandma, why did you get the butcher to cut the bone off the ham?" "Oh! Simple," she responded, "My roasting tin was too small!" As a result, three generations were still doing it and didn't know why If only at some point they had asked.

I have seen this replicated in many organisations due to a lack of a formal training programme being in place for their staff. Frightening as it may seem, many companies do not even start with a proper staff induction, even though statistics have proven that it is the first 48 working hours that can determine if a person will stay or leave.

We really must ask, 'Y do companies spend so little money and thought on it?'

People are your most precious asset. Only people can be made to appreciate in value.

Stephen Covey

Chapter 8

Ask Y are staff an expense and not an asset

Accountants are essential to a business, but they tend to see its people as a commodity as opposed to the most prized asset of a company. In fact, a filing cabinet is shown as an asset on a balance sheet, but our precious staff are shown under expense on the P & L.

What is worse in this view of the business is that assets depreciate over time, whereas staff, if developed, improve and can achieve more and more annually.

We must not use accountancy practice to determine how we think about our most precious assets, the staff, and, as a consequence, fail to invest the necessary time, energy and money which, unlike depreciation, should lead to the improved ability of the staff instead of just being an annual write off.

A frightening fact is that the cost of recruitment can be more than twice the salary for that position, to which we must add the cost of training and getting them to a point where they can start to deliver a return on that training. If they are added into a team, it unsettles the team for a while and takes it back to what Bruce Tuckman in his theory on the four stages of team development (forming, storming, norming and performing) called the forming stage. In effect, the team is virtually sent back to the beginning of their initial formation and then has to work its way back to stage four when they are performing again.

What is even more frightening is the brain drain when they leave because they are dissatisfied with their lack of development: they take what knowledge they do have to a competitor and the cycle begins again.

A company's employees are its greatest asset and your people are your product

Richard Branson

Chapter 9

Ask Y don't staff smile at customers

We really do expect so much from our staff and yet in some companies they get so little in return.

Maybe I am a management maverick and I guess it may stop me being a high-powered business tycoon. On the other hand, I can sleep easy at nights so do I care? No! But answer me this: Y do business leaders think it is OK to announce record profits one day and redundancies the next?

I find it amazing that we expect the best service out of our staff and yet we remove their feeling of security and, in some instances, even their ability to pay their bills.

I remember a scandal a few years ago in an hourly paid restaurant where the staff were sent on their breaks as soon as customer volume dropped because while they were on their breaks they were not being paid. All of it was done to improve the restaurant's profits, but at the expense of the staff. In one case, a boy worked an eight-hour shift but only got paid for one and a half hours. He was quoted as saying he only got paid what it cost him for the bus fare to get to work.

I know this is extreme, but it is a true story. I wish it wasn't. It seems so cruel. But then do those who would operate such schemes really care it they are being cruel or not? I bet you can guess the answer to that one.

The key to the best customer care is a smile on the face of the staff and the smile comes from treating them as internal customers and that treatment matches the way you want them to treat the external customers.

Let me ask one of my questions: Y did this come about? Does the stock market really expect double digit increases at the expense of the staff? If you feel the answer to this is Yes, then we now know who the culprit is, don't we?

Sainsbury's recently admitted that they had been taking their customers for granted and realised that they had reduced their staff beyond the levels that they could deliver proper customer service and had to sort out their pricing which was too high. To achieve this, their new Chairman forecast two years of reduced profit to fund the changes. There was an initial drop in share price, but it soon rose again, as did their profits.

All it took was a strong Chairman who was willing to say to the markets that profits won't be as high for a good reason and they accepted it

Let's hope other major companies see this and realise that, although the market would like double digit increases each year, it is realistic enough to know that in the long term it is not possible to achieve these increases by just reducing staff to save money, as it will be at the expense of customer service.

But, you know, valuing your staff does not just mean paying them a decent wage that should be a given it also means treating them with respect. Many staff would smile more if they were just shown proper appreciation - what does a thank you or a well-done cost?

Often we are talking pennies in comparison to the profits the staff make for the company. There is a hotel where the staff are forced to recycle every piece of paper, even paper left behind by customers, rather than print the staff rosters on fresh paper. Yet they charge £175.00 a night per room. Now if it had been to save the planet, the staff might have been behind it, instead they just saw it as penny pinching.

I have seen examples, especially in restaurant chains, where the staff aren't allowed to eat the food the customers eat. Immediately you are saying to the staff that they are not worth much. In one holiday camp, the amount spent on each camper was £1.50 in food cost, but they would only spend 95p on the staff. Hence, the food was noticeably poorer in quality, and all for 55p a shift. And yet the same staff were supposed to go out and take care of large numbers of children belonging to those campers. How do you think they felt about it?

What changed this situation? The Chairman of the company was forced to work alongside the staff for a week (for a reality TV show), realised what was going on and changed it immediately. Strangely, he didn't seem that worried about the effect on the company profits now.

This would indicate that it was the managers of the unit who had decided that this was their way of making their unit look more profitable, but at whose expense? The staff, as usual! Not too surprisingly, the Chairman had found a unit with very low staff morale. This was not the only reason for the low morale, but it was one of the symptoms highlighted.

In another case, that of a very well-known franchise that supplies chicken, they told their staff that they could not have chicken for their staff meal unless they paid full price for it.

They could have French fries and drinks but no chicken. The reason again was cost saving.

And what happened? The staff stole the chicken because they couldn't really afford to pay for it. So now, not only had management shown the staff what little regard they had for them, but they had also turned normal kids, who probably would never have thought of stealing anything else, into thieves who were in danger of being fired for Gross Misconduct, which could affect their working career for ever.

For a saving of just £1.00 per person per shift, they totally de-motivated their staff members.

Every time I tell people some of these stories, I get told countless more. I have recently been told about managers of a multi-million-pound retail unit who couldn't approve more than £5.00 in petty cash; Staff who have been refused requests for simple stationery items and have been told to buy their own; And many stories about staff who have had to pay for their own coffee and tea.

To quote Charlie Brown, "*Good Grief!*". There cannot be anything more penny pinching than to make the staff pay for their own coffee and tea. Whatever happened to the concept of trying to create a brain-nourishing environment? As a manager for over 25 years, my goal was always to motivate my staff in any way possible. I cannot understand why any manager or organisation would feel that these are sensible ways to deal with staff.

Maybe you have some classic examples. If so, please tell me.

Section Two

Asking Y to Set the Direction

Would you get out of bed to fulfil your company's mission statement?

Bill Allen

Chapter 10

Ask Y does a company need a Mission Statement

I hope you will not be offended when I say that most Mission Statements aren't worth the paper they are printed on. Worse still, they will do nothing for the business, which is a greater crime.

The blandness of many of the ones I have read can have several reasons: Perhaps the person writing it doesn't really understand what a mission statement is for or how to write one. Worse, they don't really believe in it but had to produce it, either to be assessed for some form of government grant or recognition scheme, or just because everyone is doing it and they do not want their customers to think more highly of a competitor who has one in place.

A good mission statement galvanises action. It makes you want to get out of bed in the morning and launch yourself into the task of achieving the mission of the company. Looking at many, they might state some mission of the company, but are unlikely to stir up any action in the staff which will affect the company.

In his book *Start with Why*, Simon Sinek describes at length the need for leaders to inspire their people with *Why* they are doing what they are doing. He explains that everyone knows *What* they are doing, some people know *How* they are doing it, but very few people know *Why* they are doing it. He explains that the *Why* is not about making money, which is a result of your actions. The *Why* is the purpose, cause, or belief.

It is amazing what a difference it makes to know the Why. My doctor prescribed some pills for me to take to reduce my cholesterol. I must admit, I was very forgetful in taking them, and then ultimately forgot altogether. When I next went to see him, he asked why I hadn t been taking the pills. I wanted to know how he knew that: was my house bugged or something? To which he replied, "No, you just haven t requested any repeat prescriptions, so you are obviously not taking the pills." Well, of course, he was right, and he handed me another prescription.

This time, however, when I went to the chemist with the prescription, the chemist was serving and he looked at them and said, "Oh, these are good." "Are they?" I said, to which he replied, definitely and did I know What they did? I did know *What* they did: they reduced cholesterol. He asked if I knew how they reduced it. Well, at this point I was a little stumped. So he said that 80% of the cholesterol in your body is made by your liver at night. *How* they work is to reduce the liver's cholesterol producing function. Then came the *Why*: You can either have a boring fat free diet to work on the other 20%, or take the pills. To which I instantly responded, "Give me the pills." You see, now I knew the *Why*, I was motivated to take the pills.

There are two key types of Mission Statement

1.   The Mission Statement that describes a journey that the company is going to take to reach a desired long-term outcome.

An example of this type is when NASA blew up a 30 storey high picture of the Moon and wrote in the centre 'Our Mission'. No one at NASA had any doubt what they were aiming to achieve, and it was definitely a strong enough mission statement to get out of bed for in the morning.

2.   A Mission Statement can define the purpose or broader goal for being in existence or in the business and can remain the same for decades if crafted well, and if it inspires people.

An example of the second type is the one that Steve Jobs wrote when he started the now iconic Apple company. His Mission Statement was: "To make a contribution to the world by making tools for the mind that advance humankind."

Putting it into black and white has the most amazing effect of galvanising all the resources and people to make it happen.

Now, we must be clear that Mission Statements do not detail the path to get to the end of the mission or to achieve their purpose. They tell you what the desired outcome is so that you can plan how to get there.

Showing a picture of the Moon did not tell a mechanic in the engine factory what he needed to do to make it happen. What it did do was ensure that every member of every part of NASA knew why they were doing what they were doing. By having this in place they answered the question in advance as to Y the man was tooling the part he was working on, in a factory in the middle of somewhere in America.

If your company or you personally do not have a mission statement then it is worth taking the time to prepare one whether it is one with a journey attached or one which sets a strong purpose. You will need to think about five key areas

　　Ⓨ do we do what we do?
　　Ⓨ do we do it the way we do?
　　Ⓨ does it benefit our customers?
　　Ⓨ does it bring value?
　　Ⓨ is it important?

An example of this is the Mission Statement of Ben & Jerry which set the company above all other ice cream companies by becoming a cause-related organisation: "*To make, distribute & sell the finest quality all-natural ice cream & euphoric concoctions with a continued commitment to incorporating wholesome, natural ingredients and promoting business practices that respect the Earth and the Environment.*"

Amazon, on the other hand, put the customer first: "*To be the most customer-centric company in the world, where people can find and discover anything they want to buy online.*" (As at 20 Mar 2017)

eBay wanted to give a greater purpose to their company than just being a market seller (on-line) which, in reality, is what they are: "*At eBay, our mission is to provide a global online marketplace where practically anyone can trade practically anything, enabling economic opportunity around the world.*"

Founded in 2004, Facebook's mission was the start of a journey and therefore the Mission Statement reads that way: "*To give people the power to share and make the world more open and connected. People [will] use Facebook to stay connected with friends and family, to discover what's going on in the world, and to share and express what matters to them.*" Clearly they have achieved this mission and whilst it does state its purpose, do not be too surprised if it is updated in the near future.

Here are some really excellent examples of Mission Statements from some of the bigger corporations around the World. You will notice Y they do what they do in each.

- Starbucks: "*To inspire and nurture the human spirit one person, one cup and one neighborhood at a time.*"
- McDonald's: "*Our customers' favourite place and way to eat and drink. Our worldwide operations are aligned around a global strategy called the Plan to Win, which center on an exceptional customer experience People, Products, Place, Price and Promotion.*"
- Ikea: "*To create a better everyday life for the many people.*"
- Dell: "*Our mission is to be the most successful IT systems company in the world by delivering the best customer experience in all markets we serve.*"
- Google: "*To organize the world's information and make it universally accessible and useful.*"
- Microsoft: "*Our mission and values are to help people and businesses throughout the world realize their full potential.*"

Without Vision the people perish

Proverbs 29:18

Chapter 11

Ask Y do we need a Vision

Having a company or personal vision is almost more important than having a Mission Statement.

What a claim when I have just spent the last chapter telling you of the essential need for a Mission Statement. Well, I am not changing my mind or lessening the impact of the Mission Statement.

But a good Mission Statement should give us the target to aim for and if it is a statement that includes a journey then the journey could take ten, twenty or even thirty years and it is very hard to maintain, or for it to inspire actions when it is that far away. If it is a mission with a powerful purpose attached then, equally, people need to be motivated to achieve that purpose.

We spoke in the last chapter about NASA setting their Mission Statement to go to the Moon. This took nearly twelve years to achieve and along the way they would have set visions in place for each of the big areas of the technical developments needed.

However, the most famous of the Vision statements came in 1962 when President Kennedy uttered the immortal words, *"We will put a man on the Moon by the end of the decade and bring him back safely".*

Now, do you think President Kennedy did anything to make

it happen? No, that was achieved by the hundreds and thousands of people who worked for NASA and their suppliers.

The speech by President Kennedy galvanised the final efforts and budgets required to develop the technology needed to get to the Moon and back and, unless you are a conspiracy theorist, they achieved it on the 20th of July 1969.

That is the key to a Vision: it galvanises action but can be put in place by a person who will not make it happen. If I were the one to make it happen, I would not need to communicate with anyone as I would, hopefully, be sufficiently excited and motivated about my own idea for that alone to make me want to achieve it. But, if I need to rely on others, I must inspire them to be as excited as I am about the concept or project.

Therefore, the idea behind a Vision Statement is to give the people around you the idea of where we can get to and, hopefully, provoke their emotions and passions for the idea or cause.

Proof of this was the Vision statements made by Martin Luther King in his famous 'I have a dream, that all men will be equal' speech. Although the first part is more of a mission statement (it will be a very long time before all men will be equal), throughout the speech he states visions that could be fulfilled, like

> *I have a dream that one day on the red hills of Georgia, the sons of former slaves and the sons of former slave owners will be able to sit down together at the table of brotherhood.*

With America having elected its first President from the black community, you can tell what a difference a powerfully delivered vision can make.

Now, what links both JFK and Martin Luther is that they were both assassinated before they could live to see their vision fulfilled but the vision lived on without them as it stirred sufficient emotion in those who heard it to ensure its completion.

A vision must be clear for all to understand; it must invoke action, stir passions, build up emotions and, where possible, be visually represented.

Jack Canfield in his highly recommended book *The Success Principles* quotes the story of an American footballer who was moving into his new house. As they were unpacking, his son found in a box some boards with what looked like collages on them. He asked his father what the boards were and was told that they were (the father's) Vision Boards which he had made at the start of his career. On the boards it showed pictures that had been cut from various sources like magazines and leaflets showing what the footballer hoped to achieve or acquire in his life. As he looked at the boards, the footballer apparently burst into tears as he saw on them the house he was moving into and realised that he had achieved one of his major dreams.

This shows the power of illustrating your vision. I accept it is harder to put pictures to intangibles like the feelings of safety and security, but certainly there is no excuse for failing to put pictures to financial and profit targets, even if it is just showing graphs of forecasts.

For inspiration you can type 'Vision Statement' into Google Images and you will see thousands of sites showing efforts that companies, and sometimes people, have made to illustrate their vision statements.

A good vision statement should be:

- Short
- Highly valued
- Shared
- Challenging
- Believable
- Touched by imagery
- Constant
- Emphasised

However, like a mission statement, a vision statement does not necessarily galvanise action the next three stages of goals, objectives and tasks are just as crucial, as a vision without action is just a day dream.

Here are some questions for you:
- Do you have a strong personal vision?
- Is it in writing or in your head?
- Is it pictorial?
- Does it excite you?
- Have you broken it down into goals, objectives and tasks?

What about your company:

- Does your company have a Vision Statement?
- Is it clear?
- Is it being communicated effectively to everyone?
- Does your team have its own vision?
- Have you made it clear to everyone in your team?

- Do you have goals, objectives and tasks that break it down?
- Does your company vision bring you any closer to your personal vision?

*The most important thing about goals
is having one*

Geoffrey F Albert

Chapter 12

Ask 𝕐 do we need goals, objectives and tasks

I never fail to be amazed by the number of people I teach who when asked about goals either say they don't have any or, and this could really be to hide the fact that they don't have any, say they do but that they are in their head.

Assuming they are being truthful, one thing we have always found within a few minutes of the question being asked is that they really couldn't have achieved these goals because, by not writing them down, they have not analysed them, broken them down into objectives or created the tasks to achieve them.

A Vision must be broken down into goals or it will never be achieved except by accident and, if by accident, the outcome is unlikely to be as good as it could have been. There is a Chinese proverb which says, '*If you don't know where you are going, any road can get you there*'.

If we revisit the NASA mission to the moon, I assume that one of the first vision steps was to get a man into space. They had achieved that by sending Alan Shepard into space on the 5th May 1961 just a few weeks before the President stated the final vision of going to the moon and back by the end of the decade.

Stating a vision (and even a mission) doesn't mean that everyone can see immediately the steps and stages to achieve it. Equally, and this is very important, where you may have one mission (going to the Moon) once you start the journey you will not only have multiple vision steps along the road, but also there is likely to be several visions that have to be made relevant to a particular department or person. It starts by asking 𝕐 do they need to be involved so that it can be explained to them to get their buy in.

Even a good vision, however, doesn't explain what a person must do tomorrow to start to fulfil the vision. Visions by their nature are in too broad a language to include specific steps. That is why the next stage is to break down each vision into goals.

> *I keep six honest serving men*
> *(they taught me all I knew);*
> *Theirs names are What and Why and When*
> *and How and Where and Who.*
>
> Rudyard Kipling

To achieve this there is a great technique coined by the author and poet Rudyard Kipling that he called his 'six honest serving men'. It starts with *What* do we need to do followed by *Why* do we need to do it. This is followed smartly by *When* do we need to achieve it by, *How* are we going to achieve it and finally *Where* will we do it and *Who* will be involved. By answering these six questions, it is possible to set very well-defined goals.

Now, I am not a NASA technician, so this next bit is an assumption but hopefully a fairly educated one.

One of the departments would have been given the vision to

develop the rockets needed. Now it needs to be broken into goals and I have presumed that Team A would need to develop the stable fuel, Team B the rocket design, Team C the electronics, and team D the engine construction.

Does this sound familiar in the ways that companies develop goals? It is a fairly standard concept, but I have to tell you if they stop there then generally the goals will not be achieved. You may remember the great five-year plans that the old USSR would issue. The problem was that they had to keep reissuing them nearly every year because they could already tell they were failing to meet their goals.

So, let's ask our question, *Y was it not enough to give some very bright people goals and then leave them to it*?

People are funny things, and I count myself in this. We need to be challenged and pressured to get things done. We don't naturally break down time into parts and pace ourselves over the time available. The obvious way is to break down the project and work steadily over this. Unfortunately, without the pressure of the deadline we usually find it hard to get started and before we know it the three-year goal has only two and half years left, or worse.

The cure for this is ensuring that we break the goal down into two further stages, which are objectives and tasks.

Objectives are generally set for a period of no longer than a year, primarily for the reason that they can be used within an annual performance review to get the buy-in from the person who would be judged on their outcomes. So, taking team A above, whose goal is to create a stable fuel for the engine, their task would be to narrow down the choice of fuel by the end of the year. This would then be further broken down into 90-day tasks, the first being to produce a list of suppliers for a short-list and then by the end of the second 90 days they could be undertaking test burns, and by the end of the third 90 days they could have decided on the final fuel and then spend the time that is left developing it to the point where it would power the rocket. So, to get the first task underway they would need to identify suitable suppliers and get samples.

Here is a frightening thought: If this were a true example and the person who was set the goal for Team A had failed to follow through and make those calls to the suppliers, then the mission to the Moon might never have happened.

Many companies I have consulted with have an idea about their mission and vision, but it is not fully broken down to the final task stage. Equally, I know companies that have honed their ability to set goals and achieve good outputs from their objectives and tasks, but do not really have a mission or vision for the future. They are merely reactive to the market and can soon be overtaken.

However, this does not just apply to business; it can and should be used in your personal life.

I was teaching this to a group and one of the delegates asked for help. He couldn't quite get his head around all the stages. I asked him if he had something in mind and he said it was a personal dream of his to own a vintage motorbike.

I asked him how long had he wanted to own one? He said, "Ten years", so I asked him if he had asked himself Ỿ he hadn't managed to buy it yet.

He hadn't up until now but wondered if it was because he had failed to put it in writing and, therefore, hadn't been able to analyse it and set the course to achieve it

I said it was almost certain and asked him if he had pictured himself riding it and did he have a photograph of the bike he wanted.

He did, so I said in that case he had got it in pictorial form and, therefore, had his Vision. He asked, "Well then why am I no closer to getting it?"

This was when I was able to prove to him that a Vision without the rest of the stages will fail just as much as not having a vision in the first place.

First, we ascertained that he could afford around a thousand pounds a year and so we made it a five-year goal as the bike cost around £5,000.

He had already reached that conclusion, but couldn't understand why, if he could afford the £1,000 a year, he hadn't managed to buy one by now.

I said, "Well, let's look at it this way: Have you ever thought of the £1,000 as a twelve-month objective?" He said that he hadn't up until now. I said, "OK, so you should have last year's £1,000 to get started."

He said he hadn't got it any more. I asked him why?

He said, "I don't know. I guess I spent it." I said, "OK, let's break it down into the task step. How much is it weekly?" We rounded it to £20.00 a week. I asked where the twenty pounds was going. He said, "Probably in the pub." I said, "Well they will continue to do so until you set a task for the £20.00   .

He asked, "What do you mean?" and I answered, "If you don't have a deposit account, go set one up and transfer the £20.00 each week straight into your account. If you do that you will have your vintage motorbike in five years." He said, "It can't be that simple!" I said, "It is. You just never had an action step to enable you to fulfil your vision."

I trained him two and half years later and asked him how he was doing saving for his bike, and to my surprise he said he had got it!

I said, "But you should still be two and half years away." He replied, "I know but when I started saving I realised I could afford £40.00 a week." I said, "That's great but that should mean you are just about due to get it." "I know", he said, "But when I got to this year, I thought, "Do I want a foreign holiday, or to ride around England on my bike?" so I bought it."

Now this shows the power of the Vision, especially when it has been broken down to a starting step. You start to make choices and decisions you wouldn't have made before and they get more intense the closer the vision becomes.

I hope as a result of these couple of chapters that, if you have not already done so, you will start to prepare your own Mission Statements, Visions, Goals, Objectives, and Tasks.

Start with the question, *Y do I need to change*?

Here are two answers to help you with feeling the need to prepare these:

1.	Perhaps, to paraphrase Einstein, the definition of madness is doing the same things we've done for the last five years for the next five years and expecting the outcome to be different.

2.	If you haven't got a goal, how can you achieve it?

I hope you will see that it is essential to be striving in control of your future rather than being like the tumble weed, blown wherever the winds of change take you.

Remember: Unless you break your mission down into all of its steps and stages to identify the first action task, your journey will never begin.

Try to make them as visual as possible and, if you can, make them into vision boards that you can put in a prominent location.

Section Three

Asking $\mathbb{Y}$ for Leaders and Managers

The inability to delegate is one of the biggest problems I see with managers at all levels.

Eli Broad

Chapter 13

Ask 𝕐 are we reluctant to delegate or empower

It is easier to do it myself, it will be done quicker, and I know it will be done right. This statement may resonate with you, and certainly will resonate with those who are not developing their skill in releasing work to others and empowering them.

The additional statement that needs to be added to the thought above is that, whilst it might be easier, faster, and done to your liking, you will be doing it forever.

It is not unusual for a manager to delegate a task that is above the competence at that time of the person to whom it is given and it goes wrong, hurting both parties. This hurt can become a barrier to trying again and will hold back both the development of the person who got it wrong and the manager who needs to expand their activities but cannot do so as they have already reached their capacity.

To empower someone, we must know their development level, their skill set, the joint levels of trust between the two parties, their behavioural fit for the task and, most importantly, their willingness to accept accountability.

It is the role of the manager to assess their team members in each of these five areas. Once they have established the person's suitability, they must work past their own reluctance to delegate or empower their team members. That will aid the team member's development and, at the same time, reduce the amount of work the manager must do, so that they can concentrate on the more important aspects of their job.

Meetings should be like salt - a spice sprinkled carefully to enhance a dish, not poured recklessly over every fork-ful. Too much salt destroys a dish. Too many meetings destroy morale and motivation.

Jason Fried

Chapter 14

Ask 𝕐 are we having this meeting

Have you heard that meetings are a place where minutes are taken - and hours lost?

I cannot tell you the number of hours I have wasted in my life sitting in meetings with no real purpose other than to fulfil the requirement of holding a "weekly meeting". Multi-nationals are the worst for this - they send out policies on how and when teams must meet, and the favourite is that all teams should meet weekly, so they do - weakly!

Please don't get me wrong: I am not against meetings, just bad ones. A good meeting can change the direction of the company, launch a new product, improve communication, and build synergy between people and departments.

A meeting is a time for communication and the ratification of decisions. It is not the time to work through the items in the agenda. This is crucial as you cannot create and develop ideas by committee. There are too many people with too many diverse opinions. If this is needed, then a working party should be set up and only those who are specifically relevant to the outcome of the working party should be selected to be on it. Their findings can be reported to the next meeting.

Many people think a poor meeting is down to the Chair. The reality is it starts well before the meeting.

Questions that should be asked before the meeting but rarely are:

1. Ⴘ are we having this meeting? What is its purpose? If you were asked to write the purpose of the meeting as an Outlook Subject heading, what would you put as the purpose?

2. Does the agenda have substance? If not, then we probably don't need the meeting.

3. Ⴘ has each delegate been invited? Do they really need to be at the meeting? Or have they just been caught up in the assumption that the whole of a team must be at every meeting.

4. Ⴘ do we feel the outcome of the meeting will be sufficient to cover the cost of the meeting? To cost a meeting, take everyone's time x 2, as they are not working whilst at the meeting and you are paying them to be there, plus any expenses to get there.

5. Ⴘ is the meeting in the morning? Lots are and yet we are robbing people of their most productive time as the morning is generally the most productive time to do your paperwork as paperwork requires the whole brain and we have more capacity in the morning. A meeting, regardless of its level of importance, does not require the whole brain so is best held in the afternoon.

6. Ⴘ do we never train the Chair of the meeting? It is such a responsibility to chair a meeting when you consider the cost of running it outlined above and yet, despite the training being available it is rarely undertaken.

7. Y do we allow people to text and email during a meeting? If it is that boring then the meeting should end, and if it is an important meeting then "they" should be expected to give the meeting their undivided attention.

8. Have we appointed a time keeper? To do that we would need a timed agenda. The starting point for a meeting is to have an agenda and, if we do have one, then we should be able to set time limits for each point. It has the added advantage of making the person writing the agenda realise when they have too many points on the agenda.

9. Do we allow side bars or tangents? The most frustrating aspect of a meeting can be watching other people having, effectively, their own private meeting or side bar. This should be vigorously policed and stopped as it can spoil the meeting and waste the time of everyone else.

Also, we need to keep the meeting on track and avoid too many tangents away from the agenda.

A meeting can be a joy or leave you feeling that it was a period of your life that you will never get back.

Character is like a tree and reputation like a shadow. The shadow is what we think of it; the tree is the real thing.

Abraham Lincoln

Chapter 15

Ask Y is our shadow so important

If you are a manager, then you must realise that you are always being watched and your actions either emulated or, sadly in some cases, ridiculed.

The concept of the managerial shadow comes from the idea that, as you are leaving a room into one with more light, you leave your shadow behind. Do your staff want to jump into your shadow as they like your role model or do they instead want to run in the opposite direction?

I am sure you have heard the phrases:

- Actions speak louder than words
- Be a good role model
- Set a good example
- Walk the talk
- Practice what you preach

They highlight the need for consistency by a manager. If you want your staff to be ethical and honest, they can't hear of times when you managed to overclaim on your expenses or are seen to take liberties with the number of personal calls you make, etc.

Interestingly, a person can cast their shadow over a whole company. If you mention the name of Richard Branson then you immediately think of Virgin and its various companies. In the past Bill Gates and Microsoft were synonymous, as are Mark Zuckerberg and Facebook.

However, Sam Walton, founder of Walmart (Asda in England), is one of the best examples of the shadow concept in action. In the late 80s and 90s there was a focus on customer service and the novel concept of the internal customer was born.

Most major companies sent out a manual on what, in their opinion, it meant to provide the best customer service by their company and, for many, this sat on a shelf. However, the nearly legendary service levels in Walmart happened because not only did they have the manual but, from Sam Walton down, they lived the manual. When the President of a company visits a store, normally the last person that they interact with is the customer. Not Sam Walton: After he was introduced to all the staff he would leave the entourage behind and walk up and down the aisles talking to the customers, finding out their opinions, which in turn could change his concepts for the shops.

When they saw their respected President do this on several visits, his actions cast a shadow of how to be great at customer service that they wanted to emulate, and so it was not long till the Vice Presidents would do the same, which in turn meant that their shadows influenced each of the levels below until almost every member of the team was part of the customer care experience, the shadow being all pervasive.

As with all aspects of the $\mathbb{Y}$ concept, we want to think about the issues up front. So, it is good to think about the shadow you would want to cast and how you would implement it.

Creating your Shadow

Step 1: Identify your shadow: What are the elements of your shadow, both your strengths and your challenges? It might be worth getting feedback from others, especially your colleagues and team members.

Step 2: Develop your "Improvement Plan": Take time to digest the information you have learned about how you are viewed and then pick a couple of areas that need work.

Remember to ask:

- Y am I viewed that way?
- Y does it affect them in the way it does?

Step 3: Project your updated Shadow: Develop a plan to correct or implement the changes to your shadow. Make sure you have identified specific behaviours and actions that you will want to project going forward.

A nation's culture resides in the hearts and in the soul of its people.

Mahatma Gandhi

Chapter 16

Ask Y do we think we can create a culture

How many times have we heard the phrase 'cultural change'? Even worse, "We are in a period of cultural change".

Can you build a culture, or does it form itself by the actions of all those involved in the company?

Perhaps I am being contentious when I say that in my experience as a consultant and before that in both manufacturing and the service industry, I have found that a cultural change programme is doomed to fail unless the mindset of the staff who have to implement it is changed. Just saying that we want to be a customer-centric company does not make it happen.

Every company already has a culture which has been formed by all the actions of the individuals within that organisation. If that is the case, then clearly cultural change will only come about if you can get the actions of the individuals to change in line with the new expectations.

Before people misinterpret my contention, I have seen cultural change happen very successfully. I once audited a restaurant for McDonald's which was so bad that they had to change the manager. The new manager came in with much higher expectations. He communicated to his managers his level of expectation. They in turn passed it down the hierarchy until every member of staff was delivering a higher level of quality and performance.

Interestingly, they were using the same processes, KPIs and measurements, so the new level of quality had nothing to do with any process that was introduced, or cultural programme that was espoused. What made the difference was a manager who could communicate their level of expectation, reinforce it with their actions, get their whole management team on side, and then engage the minds of all the staff, resulting in a new culture, in this case of quality.

Cultural change can happen, but it is not a process built with some form of programme, it comes about by changing the mindset of the people with a mixture of good communication and setting the right example for those to follow and in most cases it boils down to ensuring they know Y they should be doing it the new way.

Section Four

Asking 𝕐 in Sales and Negotiation

I never saw a Purple Cow,
I never hope to see one;
But I can tell you, anyhow,
I'd rather see than be one

A nonsense poem by American writer
Gelett Burgess. It was first published in 1895

Chapter 17

Ask Y are we selling this

Is it adding value, does it stand out from the crowd, or is it a purple cow?

In Seth Godin's famous book, *Purple Cow*, he talks about driving through France with his family and marveling at the amazing herds of cows. After a while, though, they started to lose their excitement as they continued to see more and more of the herds. The more he saw, the less interesting they became. In fact, as he said to himself, the only thing that would make them stand out now was if he saw a "purple cow", which became the title of the book.

So here is the question: Do you have a purple cow product or service, or are they just the same as everyone else's?

We must ask the questions:

- Y are we different and what makes that difference?
- Y is our service or product strong enough to stand above the crowd and what are its unique features?
- Y does it have a unique level of sales value and is there a life time sales effect?

These are the crucial questions I ask when helping clients to stand above the crowd and build their sales and marketing around these differences. It is surprising how many cannot give an initial response. If you don't know why, is it really the product you should be selling?

Well, the sales of our products clearly demonstrate their value to businesses and to individuals.

Jim Barksdale

Chapter 18

Ask Y do our customers buy from us

The question that most people fail to ask themselves is, "Y do our customers buy from us?" I assume it is because it seems so obvious: They like our product, which is, of course, true. However, without knowing the real reason they bought, we cannot clone that sale.

Customers buy for a host of reasons: It could be price, quality, availability, reputation of the product or the company, unique features, back up service, design or maybe you have a purple cow (see previous chapter). The question is, do you know which are their reasons and, equally important, the dream that went with the purchase?

Rarely do we buy on pure fact. There is usually emotion involved, and it is this emotion that we need to tap if we are going to be able to replicate it.

Here are some of the well-known buying emotions that influence how people make decisions:

Health
Ego
Security
Ambition
Prestige
Status

> Fear of Loss
> Greed
> Pride of Ownership

The first one, Health, is responsible for more unused products being purchased than any other emotion. Just look at the number of people who have an exercise bicycle under the bed or being used as a coat hanger. Just watch the ads for a day and see how many adverts use the emotion of Health to convince people to buy.

Fear of Loss has convinced many buyers to pay a higher price for the product they have been offered as they trust the dealer. Equally, Security is a big part of the emotions, as well, and when linked to fear of loss can be very powerful.

Pride is another emotion that works in the selling arena, especially when people feel the need to keep up with the Joneses.

These nine are only a small list of the emotions that affect a purchase decision. We must understand them and ensure we build our micro scripts (see next chapter) around them.

So here are a group of questions you might like to ask yourself, which are all subsets of the main question:

- Why was our product chosen over the competitor's and which of our key selling points tipped the balance in our favour?
- How did we meet the customer's need with our product offering, and what were the key reasons they gave for why it met that need?
- Was the demographic of the customer important and do we fit a specific demographic, like:

- Age or size of company
- Financial consideration
- Geography

Once you have thought about the reasons behind the sales you have made, then it is time to ask:

- Y do they need it?
- Y do they really want it?
- Y should they choose ours?
- Y is our sales value better than our competitors'?

Can you answer these points instantly? If you can, then well done. If not, hopefully you will have realised as you were thinking about the questions that these are answers you really need to have before you can prepare what you are going to say to a customer and how you will say it.

All wealth is the product of labour.

John Locke

Chapter 19

Ask Y we should use micro scripts

What is a micro script? It is taking a key point of your offering and writing the perfect description of it using the least amount of words. It uses the most emotional language possible and is built around the benefits the customer will gain from it to enhance their need to have it.

"I know my product", said Joe, the ever-eager, but lazy, salesperson, "Why do I need to stop and create micro scripts? Surely it will all sound scripted and the customer will know I am using a script?"

Joe was totally right and totally wrong. How can he be right and wrong at the same time you may be asking? Simple. You must never use a full script as not only will it sound scripted and false, but rarely does a customer follow their part of it, making the whole technique useless.

So, what is the correct way of being scripted? It is the art of writing and using micro scripts.

This gives you the flexibility to insert all the micro scripts you have created into the sales conversation as appropriate, but you must know them so well that there is no way that the customer can tell you are using them.

An example of this flexibility is, when you are selling a very technical product, and you have found that it is better to start by describing some of the great features and benefits but before you get the chance, the customer starts on the technical aspects. Using micro scripts, you just go with the flow of the customers wishes and use the different scripts that describe each of the technical issues raised.

We need to create our micro scripts and then commit them to memory so they never look pre-prepared.

Words are so important in the sales process that they are taken for granted by most sales people. I am reminded of the salesman who was at a party, standing there with a drink in hand, when someone came up to him and asked what he did for a living. "I sell life insurance," he said and almost immediately a five-mile exclusion zone formed around him, and he was left standing on his own for the rest of the evening. I only said four words, he thought. It must be something in the words I used.

The following week he was at another party (quite a party animal, obviously!) and this time when someone came up to him to ask what he did, he said, "I buy life insurance". The other person's curiosity being raised, they said they'd never heard of anyone buying life insurance for a living!

Instantly, the salesman responded that there was some really good insurance out there but also stuff that was overpriced or inadequate. In some cases, the client wasn't even properly insured. His job was to know the good stuff from the bad and make sure he was buying the best for his clients for the money. As an expert, people asked him to buy insurance for them. "Would you like me to buy some for you?"

What a difference the change of one word made from "selling" insurance, to "buying" insurance.

Words have such power that we really must not take selling for granted. Any salesperson should take the time to review not only what they are saying about the products but, more importantly, how they are saying it to make certain it has maximum impact.

As an example, I was working with an under-floor heating company which regularly interacted with their clients, either when they phoned in, or on stands at the exhibitions they attended regularly.

When they were called or greeted, they would always say, very politely, "Thank you for your interest in under floor heating. How may I direct you?" or on the stand, "How may I help you?"

Now, there is nothing wrong with this statement, but it does not sell anything, and they were losing an opportunity to plant some key benefits.

After a little work where we looked at those key benefits, we settled on adding two of them to the statement and then turned it into a micro script:

> *"Thank you for your interest in investing in the luxury of under floor heating. How may I direct your call?"*

Or on a stand:

> *"I see you are interested in investing in the luxury of under floor heating. Let me show you our system in operation."*

You can no doubt see the added benefits, both of which are true. It is an investment as it either helps a house keep its value or increases it, and the feeling underfoot, especially on a cold day, is truly amazing. We could also have worked with the benefits to allergy sufferers but that would not have had universal appeal.

It takes effort to create the micro scripts, then to test them and finally commit them to memory, but it is time well spent.

Have you thought about how you describe *your* product?

Let us never negotiate out of fear, but let us never fear to negotiate.

John F Kennedy

Chapter 20

Ask 𝕐 before negotiating

It has to be the most important word in the art of negotiating and influencing and yet probably the least used.

𝕐 should they agree? Equally, 𝕐 should we?

It has always amazed me how few have tried to analyse this point before going into a negotiation. To me, it seems so obvious because how can I possibly prepare without this conjecture?

If you want to win, it is essential to prepare because in most negotiations it can be the slimmest edge you win by and you cannot afford to give the power to the other side.

Any time I ever failed to prepare I would always get asked one of those questions that I hadn't prepared for and, after having done the best I can to think on my feet, experience has shown that the best answers come up afterwards when I am driving away. Sad to say, I still wake up in the middle of the night reliving old situations and proposing far better answers to challenges that were put to me. In one case the company doesn't even exist anymore, and I am still agonising about it. Ok, I accept that therapy may be needed!

Now there are some people I know who are very quick witted and can think up some amazing answers on the spur of the moment. I call them fighter pilots who can fly by the seat of their pants, as opposed to the bomber pilot who has a well worked out flight plan, but these are rare.

Which are you? If you are like me, and most people, then planning and preparation are key, and this starts by asking Y should they agree to the proposition.

The Harvard Business School went further by developing what they call the BATNA - Best Alternative to a Negotiated Agreement. This takes the concept of Y should they agree and pushes it further. Before you start the negotiation, you should try to establish what alternatives there are, on both sides, to walking away from the deal. This gives you power as you know how far you can push it, and how far you can be pushed.

The Harvard Business School analysed many negotiations and tried to determine why one side won at the expense of the other.

Now, the need for knowing how far you can push the situation implies that there are some boundaries that shouldn't be crossed. Crossing them will result in the deal either leaving one side or the other licking their wounds, or, worse, no deal at all.

In every negotiation, there are four possible outcomes:

> Win-Lose
> Lose-Win
> Lose-Lose
> Win-Win

They seem very simple, may be even trite, but they are profound. If I win and my opponent loses then they may not want to do business with me again, especially if they feel I had manipulated them into agreeing.

If I lose and they win on a regular basis, it could cause long term effects to my company and, hence, could be hazardous for the survival of the company.

In my classes most delegates agree with this. When I ask them what they feel about both sides losing, their usual response is that this would have to be the worst outcome. They are right in one sense, no one wins, but equally no one wins when they shouldn't. There may be times when we must agree to disagree and leave it for another day.

That means that, other than no agreement, the only other possible outcome is where both sides feel they have won in whole or in part, the win-win scenario.

This brings us back to the key question in negotiation: Y should they agree? If we can't answer that, how can we work towards the situation where both sides win? If we are going to understand where they come from we must be willing to understand their position. This means asking them what they require to reach an acceptable agreement. As Stephen Covey put it in his outstanding book *The Seven Habits of Highly Effective People*, "We must seek first to understand before we seek to be understood."

We must never steam-roller their views: they have the right to their views, even if we don't agree with them, and they must be given the opportunity to voice them. From there we can work to achieve the win-win.

To be a great negotiator you need to be the best detective on the market and be outstanding at unearthing the issues upon which a deal can be made. One of the great tools in your armoury is Asking Y. It is one of the keys to a successful negotiation.

The best of merchandise will go back to the shelf unless handled by a conscientious, tactful salesman.

James Cash Penney

Chapter 21

Ask Y are sales people undervalued

I am always amazed on my courses by the number of stories of mistreatment I hear from sales people.

Perhaps it starts from the myth that everyone can sell, in which case I can always replace them. The reality is very different. Good sales people are hard to find and most have been well trained to get to their level of ability. I do believe that companies (and this is not just in selling) think that there is magic in a night's sleep. They must do, as people given a new position are expected to come in the next day knowing everything.

As mentioned before, the famous author and trainer Dale Carnegie said in one of his books that companies spend large sums of money buying property, then a large sum doing them up and fitting them out, and then another large sum to stock the shelves, and then no money to train the staff. If you have ever been served by a Saturday sales person who doesn t really know what they are doing, this is the reason. What is frightening is that he wrote that in the 1930s. Nothing has changed!

Perhaps this continues because companies do not really have anything else to compare it with as this seems to be the general way that many businesses treat their sales team.

I usually ask sales people at the beginning of the course if they get any form of commission or bonus for their selling;

it is, after all, one of the hardest of professions as you have to cope daily with rejection. In how many other jobs does a person get so rejected, sometimes on a daily basis. I am regularly surprised how many don't get any form of reward, but I must admit I was slightly astounded when I was given this example of motivation of a sales team: they are given their individual targets for the coming quarter together with their P45s which become effective if they don't meet that target. You really couldn't make that up. I became quite unprofessional on that course and told the sales person to take what they were going to learn and use it at a company that would appreciate them.

Can you imagine that companies are trying to grow into multi-million-pound businesses and do not even invest in the one thing they need to make it happen - their sales force. Worse, they treat the very people who can make it happen for them as second-class citizens.

If sales are not growing, it is commonly blamed on the sales team, and yet it could be because:

- The pricing is wrong for the product
- The marketing plan has not changed, but we expect different results from it
- The product needs updating
- The leadership team has not had any recent development
- There is a lack of motivation to achieve the necessary change
- Goods are not delivered when promised
- The customer database is not up to date
- No one is keeping in touch with the existing customers

No one has stopped to ask, "What would sales be like if we had a well-trained and motivated sales team?" Yet it is essential for maximising the growth of the business.

So, lets apply our process:

- *Y do we need to train the sales team?* Sales is a skill they must learn
- *Y do we need to review our marketing plan?* To ensure we maximise our sales potential
- *Y do we need on-going research and development?* Because all products have their sales cycle and we must be ahead of the sales curve
- *Y do we need a CRM system?* Because ensuring that our customers are well managed and never forgotten is essential.
- *Y do we need to offer a commission or bonus scheme?* Sales people need added motivation to deal with the rejections they get

These are just some of the questions that should be asked up front and which, if acted upon, will hopefully mean that a post mortem will not be required.

Great champions have an enormous sense of pride. The people who excel are those who are driven to show the world and prove to themselves just how good they are.

Nancy Lopez
American Athlete

Chapter 22

Ask Y do we need three prides in selling

When you are selling, do you have the three prides? Surprisingly, these can be the key to selling.

1. Pride in yourself - Do you know how good you are?

Do you know how important you are to the sales process? Most sales people do not, and this can affect the inner feeling they have about themselves. The key is to realise that, to the customer, you are the expert. You must ensure that the product fulfills their needs, ensure it does what they need it to do and, hopefully, sell it at the right price for both you and the customer. They won't get all of this from the internet.

Without you, the customer may fail to get the outcome they were looking for and, in some cases, hadn't even realised that it was the outcome they needed. If you know your stuff, have pride in your ability to be their expert.

But the big question is, have you taken the time to develop your skills as a sales-person so that you know your stuff? Have you been on any training courses to develop your skills? What was the last book on selling you read?

You can get some great emailed newsletters from top sales trainers like Dave Kahle, Brian Tracy, and Tom Hopkins. Also, you may want to check out the iTunes U which is available to anyone who has an iTunes account, and which provides free podcasts from all the greatest Universities. Well worth a visit.

2. *Pride in your product* - Do you really know how good the product is?

Do you know why your product is good? What are its unique selling features? What separates it from the competitors? Is it really a unique product in the market place ?

Many say that theirs is a 'quality' product and that is why it is good. The reality is that *all* your competitors will be saying the same. So, unless you can prove that your product is made to a higher specification than your competitors, you will have to look beyond quality to identify the differentiators. The good news is that most products have some unique features, even if it is just that you hold better stock levels and can deliver faster than your competitors. Look at everything you can do for the customer, not just at the product.

One of the areas that many sales people do not explore is the life time value of a product to a customer or, for that matter, the life time value you get from a loyal customer. If you have a product that will outlast the competition's and does not need to be replaced as often, then consider what it would cost the customer if they had to replace a competitor's product one or more times, compared to buying your product just once.

Yet it isn't only the direct cost of replacement - we should consider:

- The cost of down time when the product has to be replaced
- The cost of disposal of the old product

- Labour costs for installing the replacement
- Extra costs if it broke down in the field
- Potential costs of re-inspection
- Any risk management and health and safety issues
- Environmental impact
- Any cost of retraining on the new item

These are just some of the areas you must think about when putting together your sales talk on the cost of ownership. Once established, you can definitely have pride in your product.

3. *Pride in your company* - Do you know your sales value?

We must have pride in our company. If we don't, why are we working for them? If you do not enjoy working for them, the customer will sense it in the same way that they will sense if you don't have pride in your product or confidence in your ability. Customers are like dogs who can smell fear: customers know from your body language if you do not believe what you are saying.

We must understand our sales value, which is the combined effect of our product, price, service, and back up. Whilst you might be beaten on price, you may be ahead on delivery times, or have the same product but a much better installation team, or a great reputation for back up service. All these aspects contribute to your sales value to the customer and the reason you can have pride in your company.

Champion sales people take the time to think about, and detail, all the aspects of each of the three prides and then build this into their presentations to the customer. They are able to exude the confidence that comes from knowing them.

Section Five

Asking Y in Marketing and Customer Service

If you only have a hammer, then every problem looks like a nail.

Abraham Maslow

Chapter 23

Ask 𝕐 are we marketing this way

One of my observations over the year is that marketing tends to follow trends, sometimes even down a black hole.

When I was a child marketing was poster sites, TV advertising, radio, direct mail, and latterly phone calls. There was a cost to all this and this cost was applied against the sale of each product. It is not surprising that stores 'own brands' can be cheaper as they do not have to apply the high cost of marketing to them.

Then a transformation happened, due in no small part to the internet, and soon we were emailing customers which was cheaper than mailing, hoping they would view our website, know about our Facebook page, Instagram, Twitter, Snapchat, or YouTube channel.

The problem this has caused is immense. On the surface having a Facebook page seems a very low-cost option. Not so when you start to add in the cost of people to manage the site and to produce the good content that will keep the page alive and followed. But it is definitely cheaper than traditional marketing and for a time it was quite effective. In fact, many companies gave up managing their web site to concentrate on Facebook. On the surface savings could be made to the marketing budget.

Then new contenders moved in like Instagram and some of the tribe who were influenced by Facebook moved their allegiance. Now those customers could not be reached as easily. Then Facebook realised they could increase their monetisation if they stopped a company from reaching all their followers when they post a new entry. Now they would have to 'boost' the post at a cost.

Google, YouTube have all found ways to increase their revenues and what was once the 'expected' low cost panacea of all marketing was now getting more complex and with rising costs.

Many also failed to get the fullest data on the customer and so limited how they could contact them, especially now with the new regulations. Yet those regulations would not stop the marketing to customers whose data is properly acquired, managed and secure, but it takes time and effort to ensure it can be used and maintained.

In all of this I have heard the phrase "traditional marketing is dead". Many companies are only hiring digital marketeers, as if that was some strange being born in a different generation who understood more about marketing today then the "older" generation.

This may be controversial but marketing is marketing and you need a flair for it, whether it is traditional or digital, not forgetting Guerrilla Marketing.

When Apple launched the iPod they made the decision to

make the headphones white. This was a marketing triumph, as it said, "If I am wearing white headphones, then I have an iPod", at least until copies came along, but they had cornered the market by then. People flocked to buy them as their peers had one. This goes to the root of marketing which is to understand people and what it takes to reach them, in whatever format.

I may be a luddite when it comes to 'how' to get everything up on all the different internet channels, but I can pay someone for that, and that same person may not have the ability to build a proper marketing platform that covers all aspects of marketing. So, we are moving to the need of teams going forward, rather than one person who can do all, or we risk having a marketing plan that is skewed only towards a person's specialisation.

Two question that must be asked are: Y are we marketing in the way we are? Does it deliver a wide enough platform to reach our customers in the way that benefits them? The answers will determine the steps you need to take to go forward.

People don't ask for facts in making up their minds. They would rather have one good, soul-satisfying emotion than a dozen facts.

Robert Keith Leavit

Chapter 24

Ask Y we should emulate drug dealers

Let me make it very clear that I am not suggesting or condoning the actions of drug dealers. However, we can learn from their marketing technique, which is based on an understanding of human behaviour, already being emulated in phone apps.

What I mean is their method of offering either free samples or greatly reduced priced samples, with the intention of getting the prospective buyer interested with as little friction to the sale as possible.

If I must stop and think about whether I will buy, there is a good chance that I will pass on the product unless the vendor has developed in me the need to buy it, regardless of price. This is, of course, the only route you can take if you are selling a product that does not have any possibility of offering a sample or a test drive.

Free is the new buzz word when buying an app, even if you have to pay to unlock some aspects once you have downloaded it. It uses the friction-free decision-making process which says that, as I am getting it free, what do I have to lose? Then, hopefully, you will really like and use the app until you get to the point of wanting the additional features. You will then pay for it and be happy to do so.

The well-known 'Puppy Dog Close' is misnamed as it isn't really a closing technique. It is a marketing technique based on the principle of *Try it till you like it*, and then you will pay for it. It comes from the idea of letting a child take home a puppy from the pet shop and keep it for at least three weeks. At the end of those three weeks, there is no way that the parent won't end up paying for the puppy because the screams of unhappiness would be too loud if they tried to take it back to the shop.

You have probably seen adverts for the chairs that raise or lower for people who are infirm and, again, these are offered on a free trial. Perfume companies give out small sample bottles, food companies have people sampling their products in store, and publishing companies give the first parts of a series to make up an exotic item like a sailing boat for as little as a third of the real price for the first few editions.

Ask yourself this: if you are marketing a product, are you making it easy for the customer to buy and are you working up their appetite for the product in some way, like a free sample or a trial of the product, or a money-back guarantee? If you could, 𝕐 aren't you?

The model of Coca-Cola is local, whether it's investing, partnering, sourcing, producing, or selling. We market and distribute locally; we pay taxes locally. And it works.

Muhtar Kent

Chapter 25

Ask 𝕐 do we mass market and not niche market

Did you know that for most small businesses there is probably enough business within their immediate vicinity to make a successful company but, instead of focusing on those, they mass market at a very high cost?

I am not talking about multi-nationals, nor businesses with depots around the country, where mass marketing is actually cheaper than if they tried to market to the business around each of their depots. I am talking about the average business supplying a good product that, rather than focusing locally, is convinced, probably by convention, to advertise in publications that immediately mean they have to deal with a much wider area, in some cases the whole country.

An example is a business in Plymouth that supplies business products and stationery. Instead of concentrating their marketing activities to the 5000+ businesses within their area which is only 86 square kilometres, and which they have not maximised, they have branched out throughout the South West, they now have to have vans with higher daily running costs, and they are probably servicing a similar number of customers, but with a higher marketing and support spend to reach them.

I am afraid it is sometimes an ego issue, the desire of being thought of as a big player. Yet business isn't about that: it is about making profit that can be used to make living more enjoyable.

If you have the right product, be content to focus on the huge customer base around you, reduce your marketing costs as a result, save on transport costs and build a bigger profit in the process.

The difference between "try" and "triumph" is just a little "umph.

Bonnie Przybylski,
Projects Manager W.R. Grace

Chapter 26

Ask 𝕐 is call volume always unusually high

Is it just me or do you get the same message when you phone almost any call centre? You get that recorded announcement that says they are experiencing unusually high call volumes at the present time.

Are they? I am not convinced, especially as at least one company I phone at different times of the day is *always* experiencing high call volumes. What's it all about?

𝕐 do they not anticipate the call volumes and schedule accordingly? The reality is that they may have done so and have chosen this to be an acceptable level of service they wish to provide due to the cost of providing a better service. Have they stopped to ask 𝕐 they are having so many calls in the first place?

Accepting this level of service does not take into account the thoughts of the customer. For example, when I get the message, I think that they must be having real issues for it to be so bad. I wonder what has gone wrong?

But are they really experiencing a high call volume, or do they know that the level of support they are giving is not really good enough to satisfy their customers, so they apologise up front even when that apology may not be needed?

Can I therefore implore all call centres to ask the following question - *Y do we feel the need to apologise for our service*?

You will be amazed how quickly you will either turn off the message as being unnecessary, or work to improve your customer service.

Section Six

Asking Y in your personal life

*If you have a dream, you can spend
a lifetime studying, planning, and
getting ready for it. What you should
be doing is getting started.*

Drew Houston

Chapter 27

Ask 𝕐 I am waiting to get started

Make it as simple as possible and start now. There are usually three major reasons why we don't get started on a project, book, venture, or similar major task that we really want to do but never get around to starting.

It could be that we are just scared to start because starting means we really will have to do it. We could be putting it off with lots of great reasons of why we can't start now which is effectively procrastinating and we keep finding loads of displacement activities to do instead. We could also be suffering from the not uncommon fear about whether we would be able to do it. All quite well known reasons.

Asking 𝕐 can address these three and it starts by asking the questions:

1. Y am I scared to start?
2. Y am I procrastinating?
3. Y do I lack the confidence in my ability?

Looking at the first, we need to ask: Are people really afraid to start or are they more worried about what will happen when they finish? Do they have enough faith in their project and feel it will achieve what they want? This is particularly true of authors who can't get their first book finished. It is not that they don't have the inspiration, or the ability, but they do have the fear that it will not be well received when they have finished, and the fear of letting go of their 'baby'. The cure is for them to ask themselves Y they wanted to write it in the first place. Usually there is an emotion attached to any new book, project, plan or task. They need to remind themselves how important it is for those who would be affected to get the chance to get involved in their emotion.

Have you got a book in you that you have always wanted to write? Then first ask, Y do you think people would want to read it? Then make a list of those reasons. You can use this list as you progress to keep motivated to finish the book. You can use our goal setting techniques from earlier chapters and break it down to the smallest starting point. An example of this approach, which I personally used for this book, is to write the chapter headings. Once you have the headings and you have completed your first objective, then you could break down the estimated word count into manageable daily tasks and then write a decided number of words each day. Using this technique, you *will* finish the book.

Every author will tell you that they usually set aside so many hours each day and with this discipline they can finish any book. My friend who wrote the great book *The 100 Foot Journey* used to be a writer for Forbes, but he would commit to a couple of hours each morning to write his book. His book was made into a movie, and he has already written his second book. He used this technique - it can work for you.

As for the second: Think about how much you achieve in a day, a week, a month - the reality is a lot. So, you do not procrastinate on everything, just on some things, and over the years I have found that most people procrastinate for two major reasons: Either they don't know how to start, or they don't want to start.

Breaking it down into these two areas means we either need to deal with the *"How do I start?"* or the *"I need a kick up the backside to get started!"* Put more simply - I need to simplify or incentivise.

The Salami technique is great for simplifying as you effectively chop up the large task into the smallest parts until you can make the task small enough to start. Experience has shown that once you get started things tend to flow.

But what if you do not know how to achieve the task? Then use the whole-brain approach called the Journal technique: You think on paper about all aspects of the task and, in the process, you use most of your brain which will help to find the solution. Then you can use the Salami technique to break it down into manageable pieces to get started.

But what about incentivising? You could go public and tell everyone what you are going to do by a certain date, although be advised, when you start doing that you will have to complete it with no backing out. Alternatively, you could use the 5 Minute Plan which works around doing something in the five minutes before coffee, or lunch or your favourite piece of cake. Everyone can spare five minutes, so make them count by doing one of the pieces of the Salami, or a small task in the five minutes leading up to whatever you give yourself as a reward. There are many more techniques you can use like placing reminders everywhere, using a pro/con list, and so on. But, you know, the best is the Nike slogan, *Just do it*. Don't let your emotion take control, but firmly set your focus on achieving it.

The third is very emotionally based and you can have sympathy for someone who is concerned about their abilities. However, as with all things we do, we don't really know how able we are until we try, and we won't try because we don't know. So, again, use the Salami technique, or the technique of breaking down a goal, or setting a plan in place to allocate time to it, or whatever technique might be appropriate. The important thing is that you choose *one* technique and then get started. Only then will you truly know if you can do it or not.

If you go to a tree with an ax and take five whacks at the tree every day, it doesn't matter if it's an oak or a redwood; eventually the tree has to fall down.

Jack Canfield

Chapter 28

Ask 𝕐 I need Just 5

Do you use a to-do list and, if so, how efficient do you think you are as a result? I have always been amazed when I have looked at somebody's to-do list for a day that contains days if not weeks of work. As a result, many people find that the list becomes more of a beating stick as it reminds them how much they have failed to achieve. Even worse is the temptation to go down the list to look for the quick wins and then be able to score them out with a great flourish, whilst at the same time putting off that really important task (which can aid in procrastination as doing something, even if it is not the right thing, can act as a great displacement activity).

What we are doing is the sensible thing of writing our to-do list so that we don't have to rely on our memory as much anymore but usually by identifying more things to do than we can possibly cope with.

So how can we pull an efficiency tool out of what we are used to doing by writing things down? Or, for those who don't write things down as standard, how can we encourage a new habit that will be very beneficial? Let's use the technique and ask 𝕐.

𝕐 do we write things down? So that we don't forget them and to have the opportunity to prioritise our list. In fact, we should have multiple topical lists (like 'people to phone', 'emails to write', 'tasks' etc) which avoids one list becoming unwieldy.

𝕐 is a comprehensive list on its own not sufficient? Because it needs to be properly prioritised and the longer it is, the harder it is to do that.

𝕐 do we end up procrastinating? If we have one long list, we have an instinct to try to get some of the list finished so we tend to look for the quick wins and as a result put off the more important tasks that would take longer to complete.

𝕐 do we end up getting depressed or, worse, beating ourselves with our unfinished tasks? Because we were unrealistic in our expectation of how much we could get done in a day and probably some of the items couldn't even be finished if we had a whole week, possibly even a whole month! So, we end up beating ourselves with the balance of our list at the end of the day.

Now we do need a place to write everything down like a notebook or even using Tasks if you use Outlook. You must ensure you write down everything you think of as soon as you think of it to get it out of your head. The next stage is to select *Just 5*.

Just 5, as its name suggests, is a list of no more than five items which are in the absolute order of priority. These are not the simple things that you would do day-to-day like read your emails or keep up to date with Facebook. The five you pick are the five most important tasks you must achieve today in addition to your normal daily tasks.

There should never be more than five as we don't want a beating stick to end our day with, and on the rare occasions that you do complete all five then you can always write a further five.

The best way to record them is on a 3x5 card that you can get from the average stationery shop. You can write your work-based five tasks on one side and the home ones on the reverse. The key to this is that it is portable and can be placed in a location that ensures it does not get buried under loads of other paperwork.

Each day you need to have a new card as urgency can change the priority order of your list, and with each passing day the urgency of items change.

It is best to write it in the evening in readiness for the next day. My experience is that, if you have your card written when you start your day, you can gain nearly an hour's worth of productivity the next day.

However, there is another power to the Just 5 and that is to try to get them done. You need to become precious with your time and ensure that you don't allow things and people to steal it and that you focus daily in such a way that you can get the five tasks completed. Can you imagine the joy of finishing daily the tasks you set out to do? How soon would you see your productivity grow?

Someone I know who kept all their cards found that, on reviewing them, items would at first keep reappearing day after day but soon, when he realised how important his time was and how it should be focused, he started to see an increase in his productivity and items were getting completed at a higher rate. It really does help to make you more efficient and effective.

Buy the cards today and give it a try.

A goal is a dream with a deadline.

Napoleon Hill

Chapter 29

Ask Y I have crushing deadlines

How many times do you work to the last minute to achieve a project outcome or piece of work? This is probably the most common cause of stress and it gets even more intense the closer you get to the deadline.

Besides feelings of stress, what are the other results of this way of working? Usually we end up pushing people away, sometimes harshly, as we try to concentrate. In some cases, we miss our deadline and then, more than likely, we end up working extra hours to get the work done.

Frequently we feel guilty because deep down we know that we have left it to the last minute and it is this that has caused problems. We may even have to apologise to loved ones, friends, or work colleagues for our abruptness.

Now, sometimes this is caused by procrastination but, even though that may be the cause, often the reason is simpler: - many live their lives on the basis of working from the deadline backwards, rather than planning to do the work as soon as it can be fitted into their schedule.

Sometimes we are addicted to the urgency that is associated with leaving everything to the last minute. The other worrying aspect of this is that we are also likely to let tasks that are more urgent push away the really important tasks that we should be concentrating on.

What is the cure? We need to use a technique I call Flick-The-Switch. We flick the switch in our head and go from working from the deadline backwards to starting it as soon as you are given the task.

Well, simple though it may seem, doing the work as it comes in means doing it when you are not under pressure.

In the short term, it may mean working more to clear off all the tasks that have reached or are very close to their deadlines and, at the same time, working on the new tasks as they come in. But the great joy is that within a few weeks there will no longer be any tasks that are under the pressure of deadlines.

I learnt this technique from a Vice President of a multi-national I worked for during my visits to the head office where I taught on the management programme. The VP's office was near the training room and, like most of the offices, it had a glass wall so on the days when he was not in I could look in and see that the office was spotless with nothing on his desk.

I spoke to his PA, Rita, and asked if his desk was spotless due to a company policy of a clear desk at the end of the day. She said that,no, it was always spotless. I asked how could someone who had over 15,000 people reporting to him have a spotless desk. Surely, he had to be working on something.

She said the reason was that he was the most focused boss she ever had, and that he would complete any task as soon as it came in. In the morning he would do the mail till it was sorted. He dealt with his emails in batches and would clear his in-box each time. He made all his calls in batches and she never had to remind him to give her the annual performance reviews for his managers.

Still a little incredulous, I asked how he could be so focused with all the issues and stresses he must have to deal with on a day to day basis.

She replied that the reason was that he was not under pressure to do the work, as she estimated he was working around three weeks ahead of his deadlines. Therefore, he could break into what he was doing to deal with a crisis or interruptions without causing him any of the deadline pressure that the rest of us suffer from.

Some people thrive on deadline pressure but take it from someone who used to need it: we are never as efficient or effective as we think we are and there is an even greater joy in finishing your tasks well ahead of their need.

The effectiveness of work increases according to geometric progression if there are no interruptions.

Andre Maurois

Chapter 30

Ask Y I allow
so many interruptions

A recent study says that the average time it takes when someone asks "Have you got a minute?" equates to 20 minutes of your life gone. Can you imagine: just three of those costs you an hour!

Regardless of what you were doing, an interruption breaks concentration and extends the time it takes to do that task. And often, because of that interruption, we lose the inspiration for what we were doing at the time.

Now, people do need to interrupt us from time to time if they need information from us or have information to give. In some cases, we are the only person that can deal with it. But does that mean they should have unlimited access at any time? No, it doesn't, but we may well have trained all those around us to believe it is OK. In fact, we may also be guilty of that instant response syndrome.

What is the instant response syndrome? If we answer the phone as soon as it rings, reply to the text as soon as it arrives or answer the email as soon as it pops into our Inbox, we are sub-consciously saying to those around us that we are always available. They may come to rely on it. Equally, if they know you are always available, they can leave communication to the last minute, so you are probably having to deal with issues that are now urgent.

Basically, they have their needs and you have your time space. It is important that their needs do not take over the time space that you have available for your needs and issues. We must put boundaries in place to enable us to protect the time space we need until we are in the position to deal with their needs. To be clear, a boundary is not a wall; it is a temporary barrier which blocks access for a given period. If you turn it into a wall and try to bar access altogether, you will find that they will try to break it down, tunnel under it or, for the more athletic, pole vault over it.

How are you going to set those boundaries in place? If it is the mobile phone, let it go to voicemail when you are working on something or having personal time. The same with the text message - perhaps check it but don't answer it unless it truly is urgent.

What about emails? Why are we even checking them as they come in? Emails should be treated as you would the actual mail: you should deal with it in batches. In fact, one book suggests not checking your emails till lunchtime. Good idea, if you can, but for most that may be too far to leave it before checking.

Personally, I finish a task, then check the email previews to see if anything has a higher priority than what I will be doing next. If it doesn't, it waits till I get my five primary focus areas (see Chapter 28 on Just 5) done first.

People get nervous if they do not check their emails or texts immediately in case it is an emergency. Well, if there really is an emergency, then they should have called you or come to you in person so they know you did get the message. If they just rely on text or email, what would happen if you are not at your desk or near your phone and they just presume you got the message?

But what about non-urgent physical interruptions?

The Golden Hour is an amazing concept to introduce into a business to help with this. It acts as an interruption barrier for each member of staff, improving the efficiency of at least one hour a day across the company.

It functions like this: For one hour every working day, everyone within the business leaves everyone else alone. No calls, no visits, no text messages, basically no interruption is allowed. The only interruption would come from customers and that is presuming they cannot go to voice mail for one hour. If not, then a rotation should be agreed on who will answer the phones.

Sensibly, you pick an hour that is usually the quietest so there will be fewest interruptions from customers.

During this hour people are encouraged to make a list of those they need to contact when the hour is over, rather than being tempted to call.

People will be amazed at how much they get done without the interruptions.

What other barriers could you put in place to reduce your interruptions?

However, don't let perfectionism become an excuse for never getting started

Marilu Henner

Chapter 31

Ask Y I should be
wabi-sabi

Sometimes we should revel in our imperfection. Y does everything need to be perfect? The fact is that it really doesn't. It is conditioning that has caused society to believe that only perfection will do and everything else will be tolerated.

Wabi-sabi represents a Japanese world view or aesthetic that is based on an acceptance of transience and imperfection. It is a place where beauty can be found in something that is imperfect, impermanent, and incomplete.

What makes the most valuable stamps? The ones that have a mistake in the printing. We are more fascinated by the stamp due to its imperfections giving it a rarity factor.

Shabby Chic is one of the most sought after looks in the current millennium. That chair, table, or dresser that is intentionally distressed can develop the 'I want' in buyers and, of course, upcycling has become the new idiom in design.

Some of the most 'designer' restaurants or hotels do not have matching furniture and top tea shops have totally mixed china. It is what gives these places their uniqueness and the quaint feel that many enjoy.

It is almost a crime at how much food is wasted by the refusal of supermarkets to sell imperfectly shaped fruit and veg. What is really wrong with a crooked carrot, or a very bent banana? The reality is, nothing; it is just the strange requirements that have been allowed to develop that insist that even nature must conform to some strange ideal of perfection.

Y do you want it all to be perfect and does it really need to be? Y don't we revel in our wabi-sabi and stop perfectionism from stealing our precious time. Good enough really is good enough provided it really is good enough!

You need some quick wins in order to stay pumped enough to get out of debt completely.

Dave Ramsey

Chapter 32

Ask Y I need quick wins

As humans, we revel in encouragement and we thrive on motivation. Equally, we can struggle to keep our enthusiasm for a project or task if it is dragging on or if, by its nature, it will be a long-term project. Especially if we are trying to make changes.

Studies have shown that the final output is improved if along the way there was the opportunity to celebrate a 'win'. It goes to the very heart of our needs. In 1943, Abraham Maslow presented his Hierarchy of Needs where he launched the concept that we have an ascending set of needs which he characterised as a pyramid where each of the layers of the pyramid has to be in place before the next layer can be put on top. The five layers start with our Physiological needs like water and food. Once that layer is in place we can add the Safety needs of shelter and protection. However, it is the next two needs, our Social needs and our Esteem needs, that are most associated with our motivation to achieve. This is where an early win fits with our core needs of being wanted and needed, and to have self-respect. Succeeding in the completion of a task which can be celebrated answers those needs.

Yet it is surprising how many projects are set out that could take years and yet there are no planned points where success could be celebrated.

When they put the roof on a new building they have a celebration known as 'Topping Out'. It has probably taken months so far, and there could be just as much work ahead, but for now we can celebrate. In Italy, they have the custom of putting a Christmas tree on top of the building when they have the Topping Out celebration.

When we are working on major change that could take many months or even years, it is essential to have those quick wins to motivate us and others to carry on to the end.

How much more believable is it to feel you can reach the end if you start to see success along the way?

Carpe diem, seize the day, boys. Make your lives extraordinary.

John Keating
the English teacher played by Robin Williams in the 1989 movie *Dead Poets Society*

Chapter 33

Ask 𝕐 I worry about what might be

I loved the poster which said, "Worry must work, as everything I worried about didn't come true."

How often do we let the past act as an anchor that holds us back from changing the future? But perhaps worse is when we let our worry about the future spoil our present.

Do you live in the moment or do you let the present be spoilt by worrying about the future? Do you let the past drag down the future?

What's worrying you? Stop and consider, make a list, cogitate, explore, but then determine how many of the worries you have are based on fact, and how many are based simply on emotion.

If there is one thing that 30+ years of business has shown me is that the things that you worry about rarely turn out as you visualised them and rarely follow the timetable you were worried about. This seems amplified in a crisis when you feel all is falling in on you, yet there are usually alternative solutions if we can just calm our fears enough to let ourselves review the alternatives without being boxed in thinking-wise by the 'inevitable' path that we think we are on.

In the Sermon on the Mount, Jesus said, *"Therefore do not*

worry about tomorrow, for tomorrow will worry about itself. Each day has enough trouble of its own."

If we worry about tomorrow, not only will we have lost a vital day of our life which we could have enjoyed but tomorrow will generally never work out the way we worried about, anyway.

So, let's not worry about tomorrow but instead live by the maxim of 'Carpe Diem' and seize this day and all we can achieve in it.

Find a place inside where there's joy,
and the joy will burn out the pain.

Joseph Campbell

Chapter 34

Ask Y I have lost my joy

As we wind-up this journey of self-discovery and, guided by regularly asking Y before we set the path, rather than asking "Why" whatever happened, after the event, it is good for us to reflect on our personal state.

In this time of reflection, it could profit you to start with a review of your current situation by asking, "Y am I where I am?" Here are some thought-provokers. (Is that a real word? It sounds good anyway):

- Are you generally optimistic or pessimistic?
- Do you tend to assume the best or expect the worst of people?
- What is your first instinct: to be empathic or judgmental?
- Is your first instinct to be supportive or critical?
- Do you send out the message that you enjoy life or that you're barely enduring it?
- Do you come across as the captain of your own ship or simply a passenger?

You should take time to think it through fully. Once you have had the opportunity to reflect, you will either be happy with your current situation, or feel that it should change.

If it should change then:

- Y do you want it to be different?

- 𝕐 do you need to change and what are the changes needed?
- 𝕐 do you need to proactively change the path going forward and what do you need to do to set a new path?

Happiness is a state of mind and you need to review what changes you must make to be able to ensure that nothing is holding you back.

Epilogue

When I started the journey involved in writing this book, I soon came to realise how essential the concept was, especially when I reflected on its different uses as illustrated in the chapters. There are very few situations in life and work where asking those key 𝕐 questions would not immensely improve the direction we take. Even at the point of writing this Epilogue, I asked myself 𝕐 I wrote this book? The clear answer was that I didn't want others to have to look back in regret, asking why things worked out that way when, by using the power of foresight, by asking 𝕐, they could have determined a different course of action.

I once thought that the concept must be too simple and instinctive to really need elucidating. But I was convinced of the need when witnessing the number of really bad decisions that people have made which, clearly, they would not have made if they had known what the outcome would be, even though that outcome was obvious, with hindsight! And yet, most of those decisions would have been very different using foresight and asking the right questions upfront. I am regularly reminded of David Cameron's 'Hug a Hoody' moment and how it backfired and yet, by asking a few simple questions before going public, that problem would easily have been avoided.

The key lesson from the book, however, is that, unless we are birthing a new concept or project, where it is obvious that we shouldn't start before asking all the appropriate 𝕐 questions, we must always remember and make a habit of using the pause button for long enough to enable us to start asking those key 𝕐 questions.

One of the biggest hurdles I and many others have had to overcome is allowing the emotion of a situation to dictate actions and thoughts before letting the rational brain take control and start to question. Being aware how likely this is to happen (very likely!) helps, but emotions are strong and can easily be affected by a situation, so you may find, as I have, that you are already in reactive mode and trying to deal with the issues. Even if that does happen, the moment you become aware of the mode you are in, you must press the pause button long enough to dig into 𝕐 this is taking place and what you can do to alter its future direction.

Will we make perfect decisions using 𝕐? No! Hindsight may well show additional and significant information which you were not aware of at the outset. But as you become aware of it and asking 𝕐, then What, Who, Where, When and How, you stand the best possible chance of making good decisions based on a proper analysis of the situation.

In this book I have described many situations and uses for using 𝕐 and I am sure that you will encounter many more now that you are attuned to the concept. If you would be willing to share your stories with me, I would love to hear from you. Contact details are at the back of the book.

Blessings on all your endeavours,

Bill

Facilitation Service

In Chapter 2, you can read about the ten steps to running an Ask Y meeting and being your own facilitator. However, there are times when the decisions the company has to make are of such importance that it may be a pivotal moment for the business. At such a time, you may want the help of a trained facilitator who will ensure not only that you maximise the benefits from the meeting but also that you are left with a practical strategy to deal with the identified outcomes.

An external facilitator has the advantage over those who must make the decisions of not being as close to the subject. This means that they will help keep the meeting on course but can also ask some of the key Y questions they are skilled at asking which may not have been thought of.

The aim of the session is to build a practical strategy to deal with the necessary changes identified by the decisions, build an action plan, and ensure that it covers the Who, What, Where, When, and How of implementation, and identify any extra support that might be needed.

If you want to discuss this further or book a session, then just email us at info@tbis.pro for an initial no-obligation discussion on the needs of your business. This could be the most profitable email you may ever send!

About Bill

Bill is a speaker, trainer, mentor and glass breaker who specialises in helping companies to develop to the next level with the ultimate aim of getting more profit with less stress and less effort. His work with companies spans the four core areas of leadership, effectiveness and efficiency, marketing, and sales.

Bill offers four key services:

Glass Breaker

He is retained to look for the barriers to growth, how to make a smoother operation, or increase profits and develop the strategy to break through the current issues that are holding back the business.

Trainer

For companies who already have a plan, Bill runs anything from a single training day to a full programme in the core areas of Leadership, Sales, Effectiveness and Efficiency, and Marketing. He is also frequently retained to assess training needs and develop the necessary training programmes, especially for those going for Investors in People.

Mentor

He works one-to-one with key members of the organisation to coach and develop their potential. It is not always a skill issue where training alone will suffice: mentoring gets through the emotional blockages to give peak performance.

Speaker

Giving a key note address or facilitating a whole conference. With his years of experience, he has many great stories to tell in a humorous way whilst ensuring that the important messages get through.

If you would like to work with the Business Improvement Specialist then in the first instance email Bill at bill@tbis.pro

If this book has helped you and you would be willing to offer a testimony then please contact Bill at the above address.

Blog

Bill writes a regular blog which can be read at www.improvementspecialist.co.uk

Follow him on Facebook - his page is Business Improvement Specialist

If you would like to contact Bill directly please email him at info@tbis.pro

Printed in Poland
by Amazon Fulfillment
Poland Sp. z o.o., Wrocław

53474496R00098